MARK DENISON D.MIN.

I0172957

52

EXERCISES

TO KEEP
YOUR
RECOVERY
ON TRACK

A SUPPLEMENT
TO THE
LIFE RECOVERY
PLAN

*Because it's not enough to BECOME sexually sober
unless you STAY sexually sober.*

52 EXERCISES
TO KEEP YOUR RECOVERY ON TRACK
A Supplement to the
LIFE RECOVERY PLAN

Mark Denison D.Min.

ISBN:978-1-7375807-1-3

Cover design by Laurie Barboza - Design Stash Books

(DesignStashBooks@gmail.com)

Printed in the United States of America
2021 — First Edition

Published by Austin Brothers Publishing

Fort Worth, Texas

Dedication

I dedicate this book to the 91 men
who bravely joined me for the
first year of my weekly Freedom Groups.
It was your consistent participation,
encouragement, and wisdom
that inspired me to create this supplement to the
LIFE RECOVERY PLAN,
in order to bring lasting hope and freedom
to a new generation of men.

Contents

Introduction

Playwright Alice Chapin wrote, "How can I possibly be the apple of God's eye when my behavior is not yet perfect? Because green apples are apples, too. One day I shall be a mature September apple, perfectly formed. But for now, I am still growing."

This workbook is for those of us who are still growing, who have come to recognize that recovery is less about destination than direction. They are committed to the whole "one day at a time" thing, because they know it works.

I recently came across a new version of the Serenity Prayer.

"Lord, grant me the serenity to accept the people I cannot change, the courage to change the one I can, and the wisdom to know it's me."

If you have completed the one-year Life Recovery Plan workbook and are ready to go back through the 52 weekly topics and exercises again, this is for you. If you are committed to changing the one person you can change, this is for you.

I love the words of Rumi, a 13th-century Persian theologian: "Yesterday, I was clever, so I wanted to change the world. Today, I am wise, so I choose to change myself."

Welcome to the universe of those who choose to change themselves. You can do this. Your journey won't be easy, but it will be rewarding. It will never end, and that's part of the fun. So let's get started. Read every devotion and complete every exercise. When the year is over, you will not have reached the summit, yet. But you will be closer to it than ever.

WEEK 1
ACCEPTANCE

"Let us not seek the Republican answer or the Democratic answer,
but the right answer. Let us not seek to fix the blame for the past.
Let us accept our own responsibility for the future."
—John F. Kennedy

The $125,000 Penny

Michael Tremonti is a coin collector. Don't misunderstand. Michael isn't into paying big   bucks for small coins. He buys common coins by the roll. For example, in October of 2018,   Michael bought a roll of 1969 pennies. He paid about $10. So imagine his surprise when he sorted through the coins and found a rare 1969-S penny with a major flaw. Due to an error at the San Francisco mint, the date was fuzzy. It's what is known in the world of numismatics as a "double dye." The coin was authenticated by expert Ken Potter and valued at $125,000.

It is estimated that this coin had been possessed by dozens of bankers and hundreds of other citizens. To them it was worth one cent. Only in the hands of a true collector did the penny realize its full value. And while Michael's penny is in excellent condition, even a well-worn 1969-S double dye cent is worth $44,000. Compare that to a pristine, brilliantly uncirculated 1969-S penny that has no flaw. It's worth? Two cups of coffee at Starbucks.

Every recovering addict is flawed. We are worn, scarred, and blemished. But like the 1969-S penny, in the hands of the One who knows our real value, we are priceless.

The Bible praises the life of Moses. "It was by faith that Moses left the land of Egypt. He kept his eyes on the one who is invisible" (Hebrews 11:27).

Moses remains a hero to the Jews. He was without flaw—unless you count his self-doubt, impulsive behavior, and the day he murdered a total stranger in cold blood.

Michael Tremonti's penny is of great value, not because of its condition, but because of its owner. The same was true for Moses. And the same is true for you. You aren't of great value despite your flaws, but because of them.

THIS WEEK'S EXERCISE
10 Signs You're an Addict

Acceptance is where healing begins. Step 1 for Sexaholics Anonymous states it clearly: "We admitted that we were powerless over lust—that our lives had become unmanageable." Still, some want a more clinical definition of addiction before they admit to a real problem.

For that we turn to Dr. Adrian Hickmon, founder of Capstone Treatment Center. Hickmon holds a Ph.D. in Marriage and Family Therapy from Virginia Tech and an M.A. in Substance Abuse Counseling from Northeast Louisiana University. He is also a Licensed Professional Counselor, a Marriage and Family Therapist, and Certified Sex Addiction Therapist, with over 25,000 hours of actual therapy experience.

In other words, Dr. Hickmon knows what he's talking about.

Hickmon lists ten signs of addiction. Check the ones which describe you.

Criteria of Sexual Addiction

1. **Loss of control:** clear behavior in which you do more than you intend or want

2. **Compulsive behavior:** a pattern of out of control behavior over time

3. **Efforts to stop:** repeated specific attempts to stop the behavior which have failed

4. **Loss of time:** significant amounts of time lost doing and/or recovering from the behavior

5. **Preoccupation:** obsessing about or because of the behavior

6. **Inability to fulfill obligations:** the behavior interferes with work, school, family, and friends

7. **Continuation despite negative consequences:** failure to stop the behavior even though you have problems because of it (social, legal, financial, physical)

8. **Escalation:** need to make behavior more intense, more frequent, or more risky

9. **Losses:** losing, limiting, or sacrificing valued parts of life such as hobbies, family relationships, and work

10. **Withdrawal:** stopping behavior causes considerable distress, anxiety, restlessness, irritability, or physical discomfort

How many of these did you check? What does this mean? Dr. Hickmon says that if you checked three or more of the above, then you are likely an addict. If you checked more than five, there is really no doubt about it.

WEEK 2

BOUNDARIES

"Boundaries define us.
They define what is me and what is not me.
A boundary shows me where I end and someone else begins,
leading me to a sense of ownership. Knowing what I am
to own and take responsibility for gives me freedom."
—Henry Ford

A Second Wall

"Then Hezekiah worked hard at repairing all the broken sections of the wall, erecting towers, and constructing a second wall outside the first" (2 Chronicles 32:5).

In Hezekiah's day, each city was fortified by walls that protected them from outside attack. If these walls became weak or faulty, this left the city in danger of invasion from the enemy. When Hezekiah was king, an enemy was threatening to attack. The king responded by ordering a complete repair of all broken sections, as well as the erection of a second wall.

For us, these walls represent the boundaries we set for ourselves to secure our own protection. Recovery involves two things—repairing weak walls and erecting new ones.

Let's break that down. How are your current walls holding up? Are there any parts of your recovery plan that need to be revisited? Perhaps you are slipping in your attendance at meetings, making recovery calls, or working the steps.

And what about new boundaries? When was the last time you added a layer of recovery work to your routine? This might include listening to certain podcasts or reading recovery literature.

If you wait until the wall comes down, it's too late. I suggest you go the extra mile. Repair your first wall of defense. Then start building a second wall.

THIS WEEK'S EXERCISE
Try Three Boundaries

Your recovery is only as strong as the boundaries you put in place. There are dozens of boundaries that you might need to put in place. And each of us has a different set of boundaries to consider. While we will focus on three boundaries with this exercise, you will need to consult your sponsor, therapist, accountability partner, and/or spouse, as you identify further boundaries that will help keep you safe.

Boundary #1—Your Eyes

While we will address the 3-second rule (bounce your eyes) in another segment of this workbook, our interest here is in what you do with your eyes when you are with someone of the opposite sex. Let me speak to guys, specifically. When talking to a woman, look her in the eyes. Do not look at body parts—only her eyes. Even a glance toward a woman's body will get you into trouble, and it devalues her as a human being.

This week, take note of the instances in which you are successful at looking a woman in her eyes, and also note the instances in which you fail. In order to make progress, you need to see how you are really doing in this area.

Women at whom you looked only in the eyes this week:

- _____
- _____
- _____
- _____
- _____
- _____
- _____
- _____
- _____
- _____

Women at whom you looked at body parts instead of their eyes:

- _____
- _____
- _____
- _____
- _____
- _____
- _____
- _____

Boundary #2—Television

Television presents some real dilemmas for sex addicts. The current pop culture is a highly sexual one. The increase of sexually explicit scenes, jokes, innuendoes, and the showing of naked (or near naked) bodies and extramarital activity on television can trigger the addict into a myriad of sexual thoughts and behaviors. Most shows are not a safe place for the person who already struggles with thoughts of sexual fantasy. Below are a series of boundaries you can erect to protect yourself against the dangers of television. Check the boundaries that you will put in place.

- No television for one week _____
- No television for one month _____
- No television without someone else present _____
- Give remote to spouse _____
- No cable television _____
- Watch cable, but only for sports and/or news _____
- No television after 10:00 p.m. _____
- No talk shows _____
- No pay-per-view shows _____
- No Netflix _____
- Other: _____

Boundary #3—The Internet

The Internet is awash with porn sites. The temptations of the Internet are almost limitless. It may be impossible for you to conduct business and live a normal life apart from the Internet. But there are certain boundaries that you can—and must—put in place. Check the boundaries which will work for you, and which you will put in place.

- Get on Covenant Eyes _____
- No Internet at all _____
- No Internet unless someone else is present _____
- No Internet after 10:00 p.m. _____
- No Internet connection to my cell phone _____
- No email use without another person present _____
- No use of Internet in hotel rooms _____
- No Internet at public places _____
- Other: _____
- Other: _____

WEEK 3
STRUCTURE

"Inside the Bible's pages lie all the answers to all of the problems man has ever known. It is my firm belief that the enduring values presented in its pages have a great meaning for each of us and for our nation. The Bible can touch our hearts, order our minds, and refresh our souls."
—Ronald Reagan

Mulligan

Have you heard of a mulligan? It's a free shot in golf, claimed by millions of hackers across the globe every day. In most friendly competition, each golfer is given one mulligan per 18 holes. But did you know where the term "mulligan" came from?

About 90 years ago, a Canadian golfer named David Bernard Mulligan was playing with three buddies. On the first hole, Mulligan's tee shot missed the fairway badly, sailing into the woods. He did what every self-respecting golfer always does. He made excuses for the horrible shot. His partners gave him a do-over, and the "mulligan" was born.

God is in the mulligan business. None of us would be here without taking more than our fair share of mulligans in life.

In the Old Testament, God's children had strayed off the fairway of life deep into the woods. And they suffered the consequences. But a loving God offered a mulligan.

"I will repay you for the years the locusts have eaten—the great locust and the young locust, the other locusts and the locust swarm—my great army that I sent among you" (Joel 2:25).

Gordon MacDonald wrote, "If our yesterdays are in a state of good repair, they provide strength for today. If not repaired, they create havoc."

You and I need to be repaired. We need a mulligan. We need God.

THIS WEEK'S EXERCISE
Developing Your Personal Recovery Plan

The old adage is true—by failing to plan you are planning to fail. Recovery doesn't just happen. Show me a man or woman with long term sobriety and I'll show you a man or woman who is following a plan.

This is true in all aspects of life. Every athlete has a structured workout regimen. Every scholar maintains a lifelong plan of learning. Every successful businessman sets forth a plan for growth and prosperity.

And successful recovery follows a structured plan.

Without a plan, you go through life reacting. Recovery is proactive—always. So write down your personal recovery plan. It will be unlike anyone else's, customized to your specific needs and goals. Write out at least three specific action steps for your personal recovery—daily, weekly, monthly, and yearly.

What I Will Do Every Day

- _____
- _____
- _____
- _____
- _____

What I Will Do Every Week

- _____
- _____
- _____
- _____
- _____

What I Will Do Every Month

- _____
- _____
- _____
- _____
- _____

What I Will Do Every Year

- _____
- _____
- _____
- _____

- _____

- _____

WEEK 4
GRATITUDE

"It is only with gratitude that we become rich."
—Dietrich Bonhoeffer

How Sober People Are Different

What is the difference between people who are sober and those who aren't?

Kelly Fitzgerald addresses this question in her article, *The 7 Biggest Differences Between Sober People and Normies*, She writes, "Our gratitude levels are different. Through recovery I have learned to be grateful for each moment and for waking up each day sober and alive. When you've been to hell and back, your gratitude levels run pretty deep."

The Psalmist declared, "Those who look to him for help will be radiant with joy; no shadow of shame will darken their faces" (Psalm 34:5).

Shame for joy—not a bad trade! The key is gratitude, which turns our focus away from ourselves. This theme is captured in the words of George Orwell: "Men can only be happy when they do not assume that the object of life is happiness."

If you continue to struggle with sobriety, try this. Practice gratitude—then wait. Joy is on the way.

If you are ready to trade shame for joy, I offer a very simple idea. Make a gratitude list. Then pray off of this list, expressing thanks to God for all of his blessings.

THIS WEEK'S EXERCISE
Thank God for Your Addiction

When attending SA or SAA meetings, I often state that I am grateful for my addiction. The reason is simple. It is my addiction that drove me into a deeper dependence upon God than I had ever known before. My addiction did for me what my church, Christian college, and seminary could not do. It reminded me of my utter helplessness in living a life of power, freedom, and a sound mind.

A sign of true recovery is that you begin to thank God for your addiction, rather than *despite* your addiction.

In today's exercise, list the blessings that your struggles have brought into your life. Then write a short letter to God, thanking him for those struggles and for your addiction.

What my addiction has taught me:

- _____
- _____
- _____
- _____

My letter of gratitude to God: _____
_____
_____

WEEK 5
SPIRITUAL CONNECTION

*"To fall in love with God is the greatest romance; to seek
him the greatest adventure; to find him,
the greatest human achievement."*
—Saint Augustine

Five Powerful Words

There was a young man in the Bible named Hezekiah. He was raised in a dysfunctional home. His father was King Ahaz of Judah, who set up idols for the people to worship. Because he didn't honor God, the nation went downhill and became very poor. Five different armies came against Judah, and Judah lost every battle. The place was decimated. You would think that Ahaz would have learned his lesson, turned to God, and asked for his help, but he did the opposite. He closed the doors of the temple and began to sell off sacred treasures.

Hezekiah was raised in this environment of compromise, defeat, and mediocrity. He could have turned out like his dad; he could have adapted to that environment. But when he became king, the first thing Hezekiah did, before repairing the roads or getting the economy going, was to reopen the temple. He turned the nation back toward God.

His father chose to compromise and to push people down, but Hezekiah's attitude was, "I might have been born in the land of mediocrity, but I'm not going to live there."

What made Hezekiah great? Despite the example of his father, "Hezekiah trusted in the Lord" (2 Kings 18:5).

Those five words are a mouthful. "Hezekiah trusted in the Lord."

Like King Hezekiah, you may have been raised by a father who did not seek the Lord. Did that make life harder for you? Definitely. Did it feed your addiction? Probably. But did it seal a destiny of compromise and failure? Absolutely not.

THIS WEEK'S EXERCISE
Write a Letter to God

Successful recovery is spiritual recovery. Any 12-Step group speaks often of a "higher power," even if they whiff on defining who this "higher power" is. You cannot maintain long-term sobriety apart from your connection to God.

In a moment, you will write a letter to God. But first, let's dig a little deeper. How did your spiritual connection evolve to where it is today?

In what ways did your mother model a spiritual connection?

_____

_____

_____

_____

_____

_____

How did your father demonstrate a spiritual connection?

_____

_____

_____

_____

_____

_____

_____

_____

How have your parents' spiritual beliefs and practices affected you personally?

_____

_____

_____

_____

_____

_____

How can you avoid the negative influences of your parents' spiritual shortfalls?

_____

_____

_____

_____

_____

_____

Describe your relationship with God as a child:

_____

_____

_____

_____

_____

_____

How has your relationship with God evolved since child-hood?

_____

_____

_____

_____

_____

_____

How have your addiction and recovery affected your spiritual connection?

_____

_____

_____

_____

_____

_____

Write a letter to God. Tell him how you would like your spiritual connection to evolve in the coming days.

WEEK 6
DISCIPLINE

"Discipline is the bridge between goals and accomplishments."
—Jim Rohn

The Silver Bullet

Is there a silver bullet to sobriety? Is there one key, one thing that will bring recovery? Is there a simple fix?

The answer is yes, but you aren't going to like what it is. It's called *discipline*.

Paul told young Timothy how to win in life. "Fight the good fight of the faith" (1 Timothy 6:12).

I've seen boxers fight and I've seen them train. The fight is determined by the training. It is the miles of roadwork and hundreds of rounds in the gym that create the successful fighter. It is what is done when no one is watching that makes the fighter great.

In your addiction, you have found your strongest opponent. He will come at you with everything that he's got. And he keeps getting up, no matter how many rounds you have won. He is relentless in his attack and unyielding in his efforts. And even though you may be ahead on points, he can still take you out with a single punch in the final round. Unless you are diligent in your preparation and disciplined in your defense.

Jim Rohn was right: "Discipline is the bridge between goals and accomplishment."

If you are committed to your sobriety, you must embrace the discipline that precedes each battle—discipline to go to meetings, make calls, and never give up.

THIS WEEK'S EXERCISE
Identifying Your Weakest Link

Your recovery is no stronger than your weakest link.

Everyone has a weakness. We all have at least one habit, character flaw, or personal challenge we must overcome in order to maintain sobriety. This may be tied to the roots of our addiction—abuse, trauma, or isolation. In some cases, it is impossible to trace the genesis of this "weak link." But it is there, and it keeps tripping us up—over and over.

I have known dozens of men who followed solid recovery plans, but still fell to chronic slips and relapses. Why? Because they never dealt with their weakest link.

I've seen other men frustrated by their inability to stay on track with their recovery. The culprit? Their weakest link.

Your weakest link may be known only to you. It may fall into one of the following categories, or none at all:

- Triggers
- Certain types of people
- Past memories
- Euphoric recall
- Fantasy
- Certain places
- Making calls

- Attending meetings
- A specific temptation

Your task this week is to do two things: (a) identify the weakest link in your recovery, and (b) do something about it.

What is the weakest link to your personal recovery?

_____

_____

_____

_____

_____

What will you do to address it this week?

_____

_____

_____

_____

_____

_____

WEEK 7
FANTASY

"What you think, you become."
—Buddha

A Strange Instructor

Dr. Jay Stringer has given us an insightful book, Unwanted: *How Sexual Brokenness Reveals Our Way to Healing.* The book is a compilation of research conducted on 3,800 men and women. Stringer summarizes, "The research showed that unwanted sexual behavior is not random. It is both shaped and predicted by the parts of our story that remain unaddressed." Then Stringer concludes, "Don't condemn your fantasy; listen to it."

I have neither the space nor the training to fully unpack that statement: "Don't condemn your fantasy; listen to it."

But here is the simple application. One of the surest ways to look deep within to see why you do what you do is to take a second look at your fantasy life.

James warned, "Each person is tempted when he is lured and enticed by his own desire" (1:14). Notice that James spoke of each man's own desire. My fantasies are different from yours. There is a reason for that—we have different backgrounds, trauma levels, and exposure to shame.

You are a product of your past and the fantasy you struggle with today may be the best window through which you can view that complicated past. Before you write off your fantasies as sinful indulgences of the mind, learn from them. Let your fantasies shine light on the darkest crevices of your past that you might otherwise completely miss.

THIS WEEK'S EXERCISE
Learn from Your Fantasies

This week's exercise will get very personal. This might be a good time to make sure you are keeping this workbook in a safe place! This week's work—and readings—will require you to look deep into your mind and soul, and to bring into the light aspects of your personal thought life that you grasp with a tight fist. This exercise will require you to reveal things that even a CSAT (Certified Sex Addiction Therapist) will not ask you, nor will these behaviors be included in a clinical disclosure or polygraph.

Dr. Jay Stringer is right. He has stepped into the arena of fantasy and found that our fantasies say so much about us. In that regard, your deepest, most intimate sexual fantasies are not inherently wrong. They simply paint a picture. And it is that picture that matters.

Let's get to work. This week, revisit this exercise every day. Write down your sexual fantasies, and more importantly, what you think they say about you. This space will not allow for a detailed description of each fantasy, so just record a brief account of each one you can remember at the end of each day.

Fantasy: _____

_____

What it says about me: _____

_____

Fantasy: _____

_____

What it says about me: _____

_____

Fantasy: _____

_____

What it says about me: _____

_____

Fantasy: _____

_____

What it says about me: _____

_____

Fantasy: _____
_____

What it says about me: _____
_____

Fantasy: _____
_____

What it says about me: _____
_____

WEEK 8
SELF-CARE

"Love yourself first, and everything else falls in line.
You really have to love yourself to get anything
done in this world.
—Lucille Ball

God's Strength

The year was 1911. The South Pole was not the vacation paradise it is today. But a Norwegian explorer named Roald Amundsen changed all that when he set out to become the first man to reach the South Pole. While assembling his team, Amundsen chose expert skiers and dog handlers. His strategy was simple. The dogs would do most of the work as they pulled the group 15 to 20 miles per day. Rather than the men relying on their own strength, they would rely on the strength of the dogs. It worked, as Amundsen became the first man to reach the South Pole.

The road to recovery is one of exploration. None of us got it right the first time. And as long as we sought sobriety in our own strength, we found no recovery at all.

The key to lasting recovery is surrender to our Higher Power. As Roald Amundsen relied on the strength of his dogs, we must rely on the strength of our God.

King David wrote, "The Lord is the strength of my life; of whom shall I be afraid?" (Psalm 27:1).

The troubles of this life multiply and can become over-whelming—downright scary. And if we don't learn to rely on God's strength, we become gripped by fear.

Alexander MacLaren nailed it when he said, "Only he who can say, 'The Lord is the strength of my life' can also say, 'Of whom shall I be afraid?'"

THIS WEEK'S EXERCISE
Do a Recovery Day

It may have been the best advice my sponsor ever gave me. "Do a Recovery Day."

"What is a Recovery Day?" I asked.

He explained. A Recovery Day is one full day set aside to focus on recovery, spirituality, and self-care. The day is spent alone with God, other than making a few recovery calls and/or attending a recovery meeting. The day features recovery exercises and literature, but also time spent in a healthy place, doing relaxing activities that feed sanity and recovery.

To give you an example of what a Recovery Day might look like, I'll list the things I often include in my own Recovery Day experiences.

- Walk on the beach
- Visit an antique car museum
- Eat at my favorite ice cream shop
- Read recovery material
- Pray
- Attend a recovery meeting
- Drive along the beach
- Find a new lunch place

Your Recovery Day will look different from mine. But the basic components must be in place: solitude, meditation, recovery work, and self-care.

Try to do a Recovery Day this week. If that is impossible, schedule it for a day soon, then finish the exercise at that time.

Date of my Recovery Day: _____

Place for my Recovery Day: _____

Activities for my Recovery Day:

1. _____

2. _____

3. _____

4. _____

5. _____

6. _____

7. _____

WEEK 9
SECRETS

"If you have to sneak to do it, lie to cover it up, or delete it to avoid it being seen, then you probably shouldn't be doing it."
—Bishop Dale Bronner

Mulch

I have taken on a new project at our house. I care for the flower bed in front on the house. This means dealing with Satan's gift to horticulture—weeds.

About a week ago, as I was tending to the plants, I saw one tiny weed in the back, approachable only on bended knee. I had to select my plan of action from among three options. I could crawl to the protected area and pull the weed by its roots. I could grab the top of the weed and remove the part my wife might see the next day. Or I could do the easy thing—toss a little mulch on the weed.

I chose option three. And it worked for a few days. Then the weed pointed its disgusting little head through my mulch. So I tossed on more mulch. Eventually, I came to two conclusions: (1) I don't own enough mulch to win this battle, and (2) the only permanent solution was to pull the devil out by its roots.

Perhaps you've treated your sin like that weed. You covered it over with a little lie or alternative behaviors, and then pretended the problem no one could see must therefore not really exist. Then the activity returned, and it was worse. You kept treating the appearances until it happened—you ran out of mulch.

Eventually, you have to dig down where no one else can see and deal with the root. You will probably find trauma, abuse, and isolation there. It won't be an easy thing to do, but it's the only thing to do. There is no other way you will ever remove the sin that "so easily sets us back" (Hebrews 11:1).

THIS WEEK'S EXERCISE
Get the Secrets Out

You are only as healthy as your secrets. They are who you really are. What you are when no one is looking is who you really are.

I'm sure there are other ways to say the same thing, but you get the point. It is what you are holding onto, what you haven't told anybody, that is holding you back. You must get the secrets out. You don't need to tell everybody, but you do need to tell somebody. Why? Because God can only *heal* what you *reveal*.

This exercise consists of three parts.

Part A—Identify your secret. Write it here: _____
_____

Part B—Decide who to tell: _____

Part C—Tell them. When will you tell them? _____

_____

WEEK 10
CHURCH

"Anyone who is to find Christ must first find the church. How could anyone know where Christ is and what faith is in him unless he knew where his believers are?"
—Martin Luther

What You Can't Do Without

You can find sobriety without community. But you can't keep sobriety without community. That is one reason God invented this thing we call the church.

Many have abandoned the church because they have been injured there. But if you have been hurt by a church, the answer isn't to abandon the whole idea, but to simply find another church.

Unless you know something God doesn't.

The Bible is clear. Hebrews 10:24-25 reads, "Let us consider how we may spur one another on toward love and good deeds, not giving up meeting together, as some are in the habit of doing, but encouraging one another—and all the more as you see the day approaching."

Jay Lowder, founder of Jay Lowder Harvest Ministries, writes, "People need the church to help them grow and mature. They also need the community of others who have the same passions and experiences. These relationships feed off of one another to help encourage, challenge, and grow one another. So no, you don't have to go to church to have a relationship with Jesus, but you do need to go to church if you're serious about making it stronger."

Tertullian said, "The blood of the martyrs is the seed of the church." That starts with Jesus. He gave his life for the church. And if the church mattered that much to God, it should matter to you.

There's no soft way to say this. Unless you are in a church, you are living outside the boundaries of God's Word. But the good news is that you can do something about it—starting this Sunday.

THIS WEEK'S EXERCISE
Bless Your Church

As a senior pastor for 31 years, I learned that people join a church for only two reasons: (a) what they can get out of that church, and (b) what they can contribute to that church. And I never met anyone in the second group.

We generally pick a church based on how much we like the pastor, preaching, worship, small group, or some specific program that meets our individual needs. But church is like recovery. You get out of it only what you put into it.

Your exercise this week will be to give back to your church. Bless her in some way. I will offer several suggestions on how you might do this. Pick one of the following ideas, or come up with your own. Then record your feelings and reflections below.

Option #1—Write a letter of encouragement to your pastor.

Option #2—Make a financial donation to your church (above your regular gifts).

Option #3—Support an activity or group with your attendance.

Option #4—Visit a church member in the hospital or nursing home.

Option #5—Offer to serve one week as a greeter.

Option #6—Bring a friend to your church this week.

Personal reflections on how it felt and what it meant to serve your church: _____

_____

_____

_____

_____

_____

_____

WEEK 11
3-SECOND RULE

*"I made a covenant with my eyes to not look
lustfully at a young woman."*
—Job 31:1

The Eyes Have It

Job knew what it was to live a disciplined life. Late in his story, we read this: "I made a covenant with my eyes, that I would not look lustfully at a young woman" (Job 31:1).

That was a smart move, as the Bible warns against the lust of the eyes (1 John 2:26).

You need to learn to control your eyes for the sake of your sobriety, but also if you love your wife. When you look at other women, you are telling your wife three things: (a) you are selfish, (b) you lack self-control, and (c) you are probably even worse when your wife isn't with you.

Steve Harvey said, "A woman can't change a man because she loves him. A man changes himself because he loves her."

Here's my advice. Learn the 3-second rule. It's simple. This practice dictates that when you see an attractive person, you never allow yourself to look beyond three seconds. It is similar to what Stephen Arterburn calls "bouncing the eyes." But I put a time limit on it, so you can define

40

"bouncing." When you see someone attractive, count to three—quickly. And make sure you have looked away before you get to three.

Do what Job did. Make a covenant with your eyes.

THIS WEEK'S EXERCISE
Get a Rubber Band

As a sex addict, your brain has been conditioned neurologically to your acting out behaviors. Many sex addicts were exposed to pornography at a young age and began to masturbate and/or fantasize about it. Every time the addict ejaculated, he sent a rush of chemicals to his brain called endorphins and enkephalins. The brain, as an organ of the body, has no morality. It just knows when it receives a rush of pleasure-inducing chemicals. This feels good. The rush could be from heroin, sky diving, sex, or cocaine. Regardless of what caused the rush, the brain, as an organ, would not have a moral dilemma on how it received this rush

After frequent ejaculations brought on by acting out, the sex addict begins to develop neurological pathways in the brain while acting out sexually. The brain, as an organ, adjusts to getting its neurological need met by the cycle of going into a fantasy state and minutes later sending the brain a rush of chemicals through ejaculation.

To recover from sexual addiction, you must retrain your brain to not connect the fantasy world with these moments of release and relief. To stop this biological cycle that you have had in place for years, you will need to engage a biological reconditioning process. One way to facilitate this is today's simple exercise.

Place a rubber band on either wrist, and when you start to have sexually inappropriate thoughts, snap the rubber band on the inside of your wrist. This sets up a cycle in your brain that says "fantasy = pain" instead of "fantasy = pleasure." The body is designed to avoid pain, so this will reduce the number of fantasies you are having and eventually lessen the inappropriate thoughts, so you can focus on your freedom. You can memorize and quote helpful Scriptures to strengthen your spirit when you snap the rubber band, but use this rubber band to recondition your brain.

According to Dr. Doug Weiss, the person who commits to this reconditioning exercise of the brain finds that about 80% of the fantasy lifestyle subsides within about 30 days. It continues throughout the first 90 days. This is a helpful exercise to take your thoughts captive.

The date I placed the rubber band on my wrist:

_____

The date I removed the rubber band:

_____

WEEK 12
END GAME

"We cannot go back and create a whole new beginning,
but we can begin now, and make a whole new ending."
—Carl Bard

Happy Endings

I love the story of the little boy whose mother took him to the animal shelter to pick out a dog. He chose the homeliest looking puppy, but one whose tail was wagging briskly. His mom asked the boy why he picked that particular dog. The boy said, "I wanted the dog with a happy ending."

We all like happy endings.

Here's the good news – we win. For those whose faith is in their Higher Power, there is coming a day when "He will wipe every tear from their eyes. There will be no more death, no more tears, no more sorrow, and no more pain" (Revelation 21:4).

You may be in a battle today—for custody of your eyes, purity of thought, and sobriety. And while you may not win every battle, you will win the war. Your story has a happy ending.

Robin Sharma, Canadian writer and speaker, says, "Starting strong is good. Finishing strong is epic."

Billy Sunday offered a baseball analogy. "Stopping at third adds no more to the score than striking out. It doesn't matter how well you start if you fail to finish."

Keep your eye on the prize. There is coming a day when you will be victorious. The road ahead will be marred by potholes, occasional detours, and moments of discouragement. But I've read the end of the Book. There is a happy ending.

Take a moment today to reflect on the fact that by faith in God, your journey will end well. There will be a happy ending. For that you can be thankful.

THIS WEEK'S EXERCISE
Predict the End Game

Addiction always does three things: (a) it takes you further than you want to go, (b) it keeps you longer than you want to stay, and (c) it costs you more than you want to pay. It never ends well. You must end the carnage before the carnage ends you. You know this addiction has robbed you of joy, peace, relationships, and much more. But here's the scary part . . .

It could actually get worse.

Until we hit bottom, we rarely bounce up. So what would your bottom look like? Let's predict the end game. If you don't stay sober and live in permanent recovery, how will life look in five years? How will things end for you?

Sometimes, fear is a great motivator. When you are tempted to act out, refer to this exercise, because you are about to write down what your life will look like in five years if you don't get help soon.

Describe the end game below. If you continue to act out, what will your life look like in five years?

Your family life: _____
_____
_____
_____

Your spiritual life: _____
_____
_____
_____

Your physical life: _____
_____
_____
_____

Your financial life: _____
_____
_____
_____

Other: _____
_____
_____
_____

WEEK 13
INNER CIRCLE

"In the inner circle, we put the sexual behaviors we want to abstain from. These are the behaviors that we identify as addictive, harmful, or unacceptable to us."
—AA Three Circles Worksheet

Text & Drive

In 48 states, it is illegal to text and drive. (I won't divulge the other two states, but you might want to avoid driving through New Hampshire and Connecticut until further notice.) On an average day in America, nine citizens die in car wrecks caused by distracted driving. And while 90 percent of Americans agree that texting while driving is dangerous, 49% admit to still doing it.

So why do so many of us still text while driving? It's simple: (a) we think we can do both things at the same time, (b) we don't think we will get caught, and (c) we don't think anyone will get hurt.

The only thing more dangerous than texting and driving at the same time is doing porn and life at the same time. I know what you're thinking: (a) you can do both at the same time, (b) you won't get caught, and (c) no one will get hurt.

Well, guess what? You can't maintain a double life, you will get caught, and those you cherish most will pay a price for your reckless behavior. What you are doing is like a man texting while driving—with his family in the car. When he crashes, he's not the only one who gets hurt.

Solomon said, "You can't walk on coals and not get scorched" (Proverbs 6:27).

By using porn, you are walking on coals. You are playing with fire. Your reckless behavior is endangering those you love most. You need to pull over—while there's still time.

THIS WEEK'S EXERCISE
Identify Your Inner Circle

Your inner circle behaviors are those activities that reverse your sobriety. Most of these activities will be obvious. If you aren't sure which activities belong in your inner circle, consult with your spouse, therapist, or sponsor. While some people might place some of the examples below in their middle circle (rather than inner circle), it is best to err on the side of safety. I suggest you define your inner circle behaviors as follows:

- Sex with myself or any other person other than my spouse
- Anything that will almost always lead me to receive sexual stimulation (act out)

Check the activities that you will place in your inner circle. Add to this list, as needed.

- Sexual contact with another person (other than my spouse) _____
- Masturbation _____
- Viewing of pornography _____
- Browsing dating sites _____
- Browsing social media _____
- Contacting a former acting out partner _____
- Visiting sexually oriented businesses _____
- Other: _____
- Other: _____
- Other: _____

WEEK 14
SACRIFICE

"In order to provide for your breakfast of ham and eggs, the chicken made a donation, while the pig made a sacrifice."
—Business Fable

The Threshing Floor

God told King David to build an altar of sacrifice on the threshing floor of a man named Araunah. So David set out, money in pocket, ready to purchase the site of the altar as well as the animals that would be offered. Araunah was honored to help the king, so he offered both the site and the animals. David turned down the kind offer. He said, "I will not give God that which costs me nothing" (2 Samuel 24:24).

Many of us never learn the benefits of sacrifice.

In *Falling Upward*, Richard Rohr says, "The task of the first half of life is to build a self. The task of the second half of life is to lay that self down."

Sometimes, overcoming pornography is diminished to just that—laying it down. Every time you commit sexual sin, it is a choice. You may have the "Big 3" deep-seated in your background—trauma, abuse, and isolation. But still, every time you look at porn or commit any other sexual sin, it is a choice.

The answer is sacrifice. You must do two things: (a) lay yourself down before God, and (b) lay your habit down.

Repeat after me—"I will not give God that which costs me nothing."

THIS WEEK'S EXERCISE
Sacrifice this Week

When the disciples asked Jesus where they had fallen short, he told them that the greatest miracles come through prayer and fasting. It's that fasting thing that trips most of us up. We are okay with asking God to remove our compulsive tendencies. But fasting sounds a lot like sacrifice.

Recovery is a series of trade-offs. You have to give something to gain something. Sacrifice accomplishes two things: (a) it focuses you on what matters, and (b) it positions your heart to hear from, and respond to God.

Below are some examples of one act of sacrifice you might engage this week. Pick one, then reflect on the benefits you felt from making this sacrifice.

- One act of sacrifice this week:
- Fasting one meal _____
- Making a financial donation to a recovery ministry _____
- Fasting from television for one day _____
- Spending time with someone who is new to recovery _____
- Volunteering to do something at my church _____
- Doing a random act of kindness for someone else

- Other: _____

Reflect on this act of sacrifice. How did it make you feel? How did this act of sacrifice affect your sobriety? Is this something you think you will do again in the future? How could you have made this sacrifice more wisely?

_____
_____
_____
_____
_____
_____

WEEK 15
MOUSETRAPS

"Mankind invented the bomb, but no mouse would ever construct a mousetrap."
—Albert Einstein

The Marshmallow Experiment

Perhaps you've heard of the Marshmallow Experiment. In the 1960s, a Stanford professor named Walter Mischel conducted an experiment with several young children, ages four and five. They were each seated in a private room. Then Dr. Mischel placed a marshmallow on the table in front of them, with these directions. "I'm going to step out for a few minutes. I have placed a marshmallow in front of you. But if you can manage to not eat it until I get back, I'll give you a second marshmallow." Some took the marshmallow; others waited for the professor to return with a second marshmallow.

Years later, as these children matured, Dr. Mischel monitored their progress. He found that the children who waited for the second marshmallow scored higher on their SAT tests, had better social skills, and became more successful in life. In fact, 40 years later, they continued to live much more fulfilling lives.

Each day, you must answer one basic question: "Am I willing to pass on what I want *now* for what I want *most*?"

There was a man in the Bible named Esau. One day, he came home so hungry that he gave away his birthright to his younger brother in exchange for a bowl of soup. We are warned, "Make sure that no one is immoral or godless like Esau" (Hebrews 12:16).

Delayed gratification. It's not easy, but it's always better.

Inappropriate sexual activity is the marshmallow in the room. It can be yours pretty much anytime. But if you'll wait, God's blessings will be so much greater.

THIS WEEK'S EXERCISE
Find Your Cheese

Not all mice eat the same cheese. Actually, I'm not sure that's true, but it works for our purposes here. Ever since the days of Adam and Eve, we have all been enticed to indulge in things that bring instant gratification, but that threaten our spiritual lives. In the case of sexual temptations, this "cheese" will put our families and health at risk, as well.

In this exercise, you will deal with the cheese in your mousetrap by answering three questions.

Question #1—What "cheese" entices you the most? _____

_____

_____

_____

_____

Question #2—Why do you keep returning to the same trap? _____

_____

_____

_____

Question #3—How will you avoid this mousetrap in the future? _____

_____

_____

_____

WEEK 16
FORGIVENESS

"Always forgive your enemies. Nothing
will annoy them more."
—Ocsar Wilde

Time to Move On

Philadelphia Phillies centerfielder Richie Ashburn could foul pitches off at will, but one day he got a little carried away. During a game against the New York Giants in 1957, Ashburn slapped a foul ball that struck a fan in the stands. The ball hit Alice Roth squarely in the face, breaking her nose. Then things got even worse. As medics carried her away on a stretcher, Ashburn hit another foul ball into the stands—this time striking Roth a second time, in the leg.

Roth's husband was Earl Roth, the sports editor for the *Philadelphia Bulletin*. When Ashburn became eligible for the baseball Hall of Fame, Roth remembered those foul balls, and he voted against Ashburn 15 years in a row.

At the genesis of most addictions is trauma. For the sex addict, that means someone brought him or her some level of abuse: physical, emotional, or sexual. In recovery, one of the biggest steps one must take is that of forgiveness.

Every person who realizes successful recovery has learned to forgive those who hurt him the most.

Paul identified the weapon missing from most of our arsenals—forgiveness. His words are unambiguous: "Forgive each other as the Lord has forgiven you" (Colossians 3:13).

If you have struggled with porn or sex addiction, there probably is someone in your past who harmed you deeply. You have traveled the road of resentment long enough. It's time to take the exit ramp of forgiveness.

THIS WEEK'S EXERCISE
Write a Letter to Yourself

In recovery, it is imperative that we learn to forgive those who have injured us with the "Big 3"—abuse, trauma, and isolation. But there is another person we need to forgive. That is, of course, ourselves. For many, this seems a bridge too far. When we look back at all we have done to hurt our spouse, children, and those closest to us, we can retreat into the sea of shame, never to be heard from again.

If you have struggled with sexually compulsive activity, this is not an option. You *must* forgive yourself.

This is a form of making amends. And as with other amends, it is best done in writing. So your exercise this week is to write a letter to yourself. God has already forgiven you, so now it's your turn. Forgive yourself for all that you have done and all whom you have hurt. And pledge to walk a different path for the rest of your life—one day at a time.

Write your letter here.

_____

_____

_____

_____

_____

_____

_____

_____

_____

_____

_____

_____

_____

_____

_____

_____

WEEK 17
TEMPTATION

Why God Allows Temptation

J.I. Packer wrote the classic book, *Knowing God*. On the subject of personal hardships in the Christian's life, Packer states, "God exposes us to these things, so as to overwhelm us with a sense of our own inadequacy, and to drive us to cling to him more closely. This is the ultimate reason, from our standpoint, that God fills our lives with troubles and perplexities of one sort or another—it is to ensure that we shall learn to hold him fast."

One of those perplexities is the temptations that keep coming, despite endless moments of remorse, repentance, and recommitments.

You are promised, "No temptation has overtaken you except what is common to mankind. And God is faithful; he will not let you be tempted beyond what you can bear. But when you are tempted, he will also provide a way out so that you can endure it" (1 Corinthians 10:13).

When you face temptation, you have two choices. You can (a) give in, or (b) look up. In our addictions, we need to learn to look up. We must see temptation as a test. Each time we pass the test, we gain new strength for the next time.

Today, when you are tempted, follow Packer's advice. Let that temptation "drive you to cling to him more closely ... learn to hold him fast."

THIS WEEK'S EXERCISE
Beat Back Temptation

When temptation comes knocking on your door, you need a plan. You can answer the door and let it in. Or you can keep the door locked. What you cannot do is hide in the back room, pretending you aren't at home. You must respond.

But if you wait until the knock on the door before you have a plan in place, you will be playing with fire. You need a three-phase plan for dealing with temptation: (a) what to do **before** the temptation hits, (b) what to do **when** the temptation hits, and (c) what to do **after** the temptation hits.

Before the Temptation Hits

You know it's coming. There is no chance that you will be immune to temptation. The enemy is real, and he wants to bring you down. Your own past makes you vulnerable to certain attacks. But the good news is that you can prepare for the enemy. You would be foolish to not prepare. So what are some of the steps you will take in advance, to put yourself in the best possible position for victory when the temptation hits?

- _____
- _____
- _____
- _____
- _____

When the Temptation Hits

While there are certainly steps you can take to avoid temptation and to prepare for temptation, there will be times when temptation will be unavoidable. You need to be ready for these moments. You can do everything right, and still get hit out of the blue with an intrusive thought, physical temptation, or trigger. What are some steps you will take to respond when temptation hits?

- _____
- _____
- _____
- _____
- _____

After the Temptation Hits

At some point this week, you will face temptation. You need to learn from that temptation, whether you gave into it or not. So think about your most recent sexual temptation, and reflect on some lessons you can take away from that situation.

- _____
- _____

- _____
- _____
- _____

WEEK 18
COMMUNITY

*"God has called me into a personal relationship with his Son,
but he hasn't called me into a private relationship with his Son."*
—Anonymous

It Takes a Team

Congratulations on your commitment to personal purity! There are two truths you must embrace early on: community and transparency.

Dietrich Bonhoeffer wrote, in *Life Together*, "The final obstacle to true Christian fellowship is the inability to be sinners together."

We must learn to be together, but togetherness is not enough. Sobriety is dependent on connecting with saints who know they are sinners. Then we must become comfortable with being sinners together.

It is impossible to overstate the need for transparent community in recovery. Alex Lerza, clinical psychologist and Certified Sex Addiction Therapist, says it like this: "The opposite of addiction is not sobriety, but relationship."

The secret sauce for the early church was their interconnectedness. "They devoted themselves to the apostles' teaching and the fellowship" (Acts 2:42). Most churches are big on teaching but weak on fellowship. We need both.

Find a group with whom you can connect at the deepest levels of life. How will you know you have found the right group? They are comfortable with being sinners together.

THIS WEEK'S EXERCISE
Name a Pair

Dr. Dennis Swanberg has given us some great insight into the value of community in *The Man Code*. He delves into the example of Jesus and the groups that mattered to him on a personal level. Among those, Jesus had a group of three (his inner circle), a group of 12 (his small group), and a group of 120 (which represents the church).

Likewise, we need certain people in our sphere of influence and fellowship. You were not created to be alone, and you cannot sustain recovery by yourself. When you talk to guys who have been in 12-Step groups for years, you will hear a myriad of reasons guys are in the program: (a) 12-Step work, (b) working with a sponsor, (c) reading through the materials. But the thing you will hear most is that the men draw great strength and encouragement from being with other guys who share the same struggle.

We all need community. But not all community is good. Today, focus on the people you need to embrace in your life, as well as those you need to avoid.

Avoid? Yes! We all know people who are simply too toxic to be in our inner circle, or even in our lives at all. They bring us down. They may be bad triggers or a negative influence. As important as it is to fellowship with the right people, we need to walk away from the wrong people. They aren't necessarily bad people, but they are bad for us.

Exercise #1—The Right Crowd

List up to five people you need to seek time with, who will help move your recovery forward.

- _____
- _____
- _____
- _____
- _____

Exercise #2—The Wrong Crowd

List up to five people who are toxic, and who you need to not have in your life right now.

- _____
- _____
- _____
- _____
- _____

—

WEEK 19

MARKERS

*"Our goals should serve as markers, measurements
of the progress we make in pursuit of something
greater than ourselves."*
—Simon Sinek

12 Stones

God's children had dreamed of reaching the Promised Land for generations. Finally, under the leadership of Joshua, that day came. And they were quick to commemorate the event. Joshua told the men to set stones in place as a memorial of the crossing of the Jordan River. And then he told them what to tell the next generation.

"Tell them that the flow of the Jordan was cut off before the ark of the covenant of the Lord. When it crossed the Jordan, the waters of the Jordan were cut off. These stones are to be a memorial to the people of Israel forever" (Joshua 4:7).

The children of God still had a long way to go, but this was a day to remember how far they had already come. They didn't have much, but they were headed in the right direction.

In recovery, it is important to remember what we have already achieved, with the help of God. Charles Spurgeon said, "It is not how much we have, but how much we enjoy that makes us happy."

Sure, you still have a long way to go. But today, be thankful for how far you have already come.

THIS WEEK'S EXERCISE
What Phase Are You In?

It is important that you understand where you are in your recovery process and where you are headed. Some experts, such as Patrick Carnes and Milton Magness, have taught that the full process of recovery is measured in years, usually about three to five.

Milton Magness lists four phases of recovery.

Phase 1—Survival (six months to one year)

You are in the Survival Phase of your recovery if you:

- Have just started your recovery
- Have recently slipped or relapsed
- Have not been able to establish a period of sobriety
- Have recently experienced a crisis related to acting out

Phase 2—Stability (six months to two years)

This is a period when you begin to find sure footing in your recovery. You are in the Stability Phase of your recovery if you:

- Have established sobriety
- Have good recovery routines established including attending 12-Step meetings

- Are actively working with a sponsor

Phase 3—Sustaining (18 months to three years)

This phase usually begins between 18 months and three years into recovery and lasts one year or more. You are in this phase if you:

- Have made a disclosure of your acting out behaviors to your relationship partner
- Are successfully living "slip free," with unbroken sobriety of at least six months
- Your partner is actively working his or her own recovery

Phase 4—Freedom (2.5 years or more)

This is the maintenance phase of recovery, and this is momentous! This comes after 2.5 years or more of recovery work. Here, you are moving away from regular therapy and finding victory. You are in this stage if you:

- Have at least one year of unbroken sobriety
- Are living a balanced, growing life
- Have reached the point in which acting out has become more of a memory than a present temptation

Here's your exercise. First, identify which phase you are in today. Second, explain how you plan to move forward into the next phase.

Your current phase of recovery

- Survival Phase _____
- Stability Phase _____

- Sustaining Phase _____
- Freedom Phase _____

Now, explain how you plan to move to the next phase. (If you are in the Freedom Phase, explain how you plan to stay there.)

_____

_____

_____

_____

_____

_____

_____

_____

_____

_____

_____

_____

_____

_____

_____

WEEK 20
MIDDLE CIRCLE

"Middle circle behaviors tend to lead addicts
back to the inner circle."
—Sex Addicts Anonymous

Mired in the Weeds

The date was October 13, 1960. Andy Jerke was just like every other boy growing up in Pittsburgh. He loved baseball, and especially the Pirates. On this day, the Pirates were hosting the vaunted New York Yankees for Game 7 of the World Series. The game came down to the bottom of the ninth inning. The score was tied. And Andy was there, at Forbes Field.

Then he remembered he had promised his mother to be home by 4:30 to help with dinner. So he left the game in the bottom of the ninth, to walk home.

As Andy was walking across the lot beyond the outfield wall, a baseball landed near his feet. He picked up the ball, and a security man informed him that Bill Mazeroski had just hit that ball for a game-winning home run. And now the ball belonged to Andy.

Andy played with the ball a year later and lost it in a field full of tall weeds. He looked for the ball for ten minutes, then gave up. What happened to the ball? It got mired in the weeds.

Jesus said, "As the weeds are pulled up and burned in the fire, so it will be at the end of the age" (Matthew 13:40).

Dale Carnegie warned, "Our fatigue is caused by worry, frustration, and resentment." In other words, we tend to get mired in the weeds. In recovery, we must never lose focus. We must keep moving forward, not sidetracked by worry, frustration, or resentment.

THIS WEEK'S EXERCISE
Update Your Middle Circle

Of the three circles (outer, middle, inner), this is the most important and the one that changes most often. While the outer circle represents those behaviors that contribute to your sobriety and the inner circle behaviors are those which represent a breach in your sobriety, it is the middle circle that determines your destiny. These are the things you do that, while not breaking your sobriety, lead you dangerously close to the inner circle behaviors that represent relapse.

It is wisest to enlist the help of a sponsor or someone else with strong sobriety, before completing your middle circle list. And again, this will be fluid. There will be some activities you can move out of the middle circle eventually, and other activities you will need to add.

Here are a few examples of common middle circle activities:

- Watching certain TV channels or shows
- Staying up too late at night

- Too much time on social media
- Browsing the Internet
- Dropping out of 12-Step meetings
- An unhealthy diet
- Toxic relationships
- Time that is not accounted for
- Traveling alone
- Lunch with someone of the opposite sex
- Certain music
- Unprotected devices
- Texting with the opposite sex
- Carrying too much cash
- Particular restaurants, malls, or areas of town

List your middle circle behaviors:

- _____
- _____
- _____
- _____
- _____
- _____
- _____

WEEK 21
HONESTY

"Being honest may not get you a lot of friends,
but it'll always get you the right ones."
—John Lennon

Getting Honest

Americans lie—a lot. *USA Today* recently cited statistics from a book, *The Day America Told the Truth.* They reported that 91% of Americans lie routinely. Specifically, 36% tell "big lies," 86% lie to their parents, 75% to their friends, 73% to their siblings, and 69% to their spouse.

What are we lying about? Eighty-one percent lie about their feelings, 43% about their income, and 40% lie about sex.

Solomon said, "The Lord hates a lying tongue" (Proverbs 6:17).

Guess who else hates "a lying tongue"? Your wife or husband. Recovery taught me something that decades of marriage never did. My wife values honesty more than anything. That's why it was so important for me to give a full disclosure of my past, accompanied with a polygraph—not just once, but several times.

William Shakespeare wrote, "Honesty is the best policy. If I lose my honor, I lose myself." One of the first things you must do to get sober is to get honest—with yourself, your spouse, and your God. Until you get completely honest, you will lose your sobriety. Worse yet, you will lose yourself.

THIS WEEK'S EXERCISE
Do a FASTT Check-In

To get well, you must get honest. And to stay well, you have to stay honest. For couples who have completed a clinical disclosure, they often receive materials for follow-up. These materials usually include instructions for the couple to engage in frequent "FASTT Check-Ins." These are times when the addict communicates the status of his recovery to his wife.

The FASTT Check-In is readily available online. And while it is designed for married couples in recovery, the principles of honesty and openness are helpful for single men (or women), and as a tool to express one's progress to his sponsor or trusted accountability partner.

For this exercise, identify the person with whom you will check in. Then set up a time to meet with this person. (If you are married, this person can be your spouse.)

Follow the following formula in checking in. Remember, for this to be effective, you must be completely honest.

Feelings: What are you feeling? If there are multiple feelings, state each one.

Activities: What activities are you engaging in an effort to remain sober?

Sobriety/Slip: Express the status of your sobriety or acknowledge a recent slip.

Threats: What are the greatest threats to your sobriety this week?

Tools: What tools will you use to stay sober in the coming days?

WEEK 22

RELAPSE

"Recovery is an acceptance that your life is in shambles, and you have to change it."
—Jamie Lee Curtis

The Three Stages of Relapse

Studies indicate that 85% of those in recovery suffer relapse. How does this happen? I suggest that relapse is not some "I didn't see that coming" kind of thing. Relapse always follows a predictable pattern.

Stage 1—Emotional Relapse. The addict allows her mind to focus on the temporary pleasures of her addiction. Warning signs are isolation, not going to meetings, relaxed boundaries, and denial.

Stage 2—Mental Relapse. The addict goes from missing the pleasures of her disease to considering ways to re-engage the behaviors. Warning signs are deep cravings, euphoric recall, fantasy, minimizing consequences, and bargaining with oneself.

Stage 3—Physical Relapse. This final phase is the acting out phase. The addict returns to her destructive habits. Always, the addict bargains with herself that she will do this just once. But she discovers that she has crossed the line that Dr. S.M. Melemis calls "the point of no return."

Here's the lesson. Relapse doesn't "just happen." It is a predictable process. And that's good, because this means you can see it coming. The answer? When you find yourself slipping into Stage 1 (Emotional Relapse) step up your recovery work—*immediately*!

Any of us is susceptible to relapse. Take this verse to heart: "Let him who thinks he stands take heed, lest he fall" (1 Corinthians 10:12).

THIS WEEK'S EXERCISE
Avoid Relapse

Relapse doesn't just happen. It is the culmination of missed meetings, missed calls, and missed opportunities. And even then, relapse follows a predictable pattern.

1. We think it.
2. We plan it.
3. We do it.
4. We hate it.
5. We cover it.
6. We do it again.

The problem is really not the "do it again" phase. By the time we have thought about it and planned it, it's pretty much over. Relapse always happens in the brain before it is carried out by the body. We have sex with the wrong person in our head before we ever have sex with them in our bed.

Your job is to identify the repeated thought patterns and activities that have led to most of your relapses. And as a sex addict, you have plenty of material to work with. In order to stop the next relapse before it happens, you have to see it coming.

Here's your exercise. If you do relapse in the future, what are the triggers, causes, or circumstances that will lead you down that path if you don't deal with them in time?

- _____

- _____

- _____

- _____

- _____

- _____

- _____

WEEK 23
SURRENDER

"God is ready to assume full responsibility
for the life wholly yielded to him."
—Andrew Murray

The Meaning of Surrender

Oscar Wilde wrote, "Everything in the world is about sex except sex. Sex is about power."

Research confirms this thesis. Sex is about power. And addicts can never get enough. Many of us can identify with the line in *Top Gun*. We have an incredible "need for speed."

This speed comes in many forms—with sex at the top of the list. Like those who struggle with substances, impulse control disorders, or behavioral addictions, sexual addicts find themselves with ever-growing passions and ever-diminishing satisfaction.

This is what makes recovery so hard for so many. We want sobriety, but we also want power. We want to be in control. But we can't have both. Recovery is absolutely rooted in surrender.

How do we find victory? James offers clear insight. "Submit yourselves therefore to God. Resist the devil, and he will flee from you" (James 4:7).

Oswald Chambers was right: "If you have only come as far as asking God for things, you have never come to understand the meaning of surrender."

THIS WEEK'S EXERCISE
Plan a Sweet Surrender

Step 3 says, "We made a decision to turn our wills and our lives over to the care of God as we understood God." That is a decision we all must make—every day.

But deciding to surrender to God is not the same thing as actually surrendering to God. This week, you will take the sweet step of surrender. Now, set aside a few minutes for this powerful exercise.

Below, make a list of all the things in your life that you need to let go of, that you need to surrender to God. Then write each of them on a separate scrap of paper. It is best to do this in several settings, as you will think of new areas to surrender each time you focus on this. Once you feel comfortable that you have written down everything that needs to be surrendered, move to the most important part of the exercise.

Take those scraps of paper and find a place of solitude. Then get down on your knees and surrender each of these parts of your life to God. As you release each one, place that scrap of paper next to you. When you are finished, pick up those papers and discard them. Put them in a trash can where you can never go back and retrieve them.

Things I will surrender to God:

- _____

- _____

- _____
- _____
- _____
- _____
- _____
- _____

Where I will go to surrender these to God:

_____

Date I will surrender these things:

_____

WEEK 24
GUARDRAILS

"Givers need to set limits because takers rarely do."
—Rachel Wolchin

Close the Window

It happened on April 17, 1790. Ben Franklin died from sitting in front of his window. Here's what happened. Franklin was a big believer in fresh air. So every night, he slept with the window open. He wrote, "I rise every morning and sit near the window in my chamber without any clothes, regardless of the season."

April of 1790 started like any other time in the 84-year-old's life. But this time, Franklin developed an abscess in his lungs, which his doctors attributed to his many hours sitting naked in front of an open window. The abscess burst on April 17, and he died a few hours later.

Many of us suffer from open windows. We open the window to temptation—just a little—and we are okay. Until we're not.

Peter warned, "Keep away from worldly desires that wage war against your very souls" (1 Peter 2:11).

Maintaining sobriety is a war. It will probably be the most difficult battle you ever face. One of the keys to victory is to keep the window of temptation nailed shut. Don't even crack the window a little. This may mean you need to avoid certain places, television shows, or toxic relationships. If you allow the window of temptation to remain open, you will soon find yourself like Ben Franklin—naked and helpless.

It's time to shut the window.

THIS WEEK'S EXERCISE
Build a Guardrail

Across America, the Highway Department has erected 4,386,000 miles of guardrails along federal highways. Actually, I made that number up. But here's something I didn't make up—guardrails have saved thousands of lives. If you are a newer driver, let me explain how this works. You aren't supposed to get as close as you can without going over the edge of the road. If you do that, there will eventually be an unexpected bump in the road, and you'll lose it.

In recovery, guardrails represent the steps we take to keep us from going over the edge. Curiosity says, "I wonder what is on the other side of the guardrail." Intelligence says, "Don't go there. It's just too dangerous."

We all need guardrails in order to keep our recovery in the safe zone. These will be different for each of us. What you need to do in order to stay safe may not work for me, and vice versa. And the guardrails will change, depending on where we are in our recovery. That means that this week's exercise is one you may want to revisit in a few months.

Here we go. Pick one of the guardrails from the list below. If none of these seem to fit your personal recovery needs, identify a different guardrail. For now, just pick one, and write down your specific plan for that guardrail.

- Get on Covenant Eyes: _____
- End a toxic relationship: _____
- Go to bed earlier at night: _____
- Change your TV habits: _____
- Adjust your social media exposure: _____
- Give your spouse access to your phone: _____
- Avoid certain areas of town: _____
- Limit the cash you carry: _____
- Don't be alone with the opposite sex: _____
- Limit time on your computer: _____
- Other: _____

WEEK 25
ISOLATION

"A person is a person through other persons;
you can't be human in isolation; you
are human only in relationships."
—Desmond Tutu

Pitcairn Island

Pitcairn Island is one of the most remote places on earth. Set in the Pacific Ocean, it is home to just 50 residents, and for good reason—you can't get there. You must fly to Tahiti and then sail for 1,200 miles. Then you transfer to a ruby dinghy, take your climbing gear and eventually scale the 900-foot rock cliffs to the tiny village.

Pitcairn Island is a metaphor on loneliness and isolation. And Pitcairn Island is a metaphor on addiction.

Solomon wrote, "Whoever isolates himself seeks his own desire; he rejects sound judgment" (Proverbs 18:1).

Addicts come in all shapes and sizes. Addiction knows no color or creed, race or religion. But if you look hard enough and long enough into every addict's past you will find the same thing.

Isolation.

Hear the words of John Lennon's hit song from 1970: *"People say we've got it made. Don't they know we're so afraid? We're afraid to be alone. Everybody got to have a home."*

The facts are these: Nobody has it made, we're all afraid, we don't want to be alone, and we've all got to have a home.

Here's the thing. Isolation is not a condition as much as it is a choice. So join the family of God, get in a support group, and get outside yourself. Why? Because if you don't defeat the demon of isolation, the demon of isolation will defeat you.

THIS WEEK'S EXERCISE
Don't Isolate

Isolation is not your friend. While it is healthy to schedule "alone" times, you cannot maintain sobriety apart from the fellowship of others. You need to be a part of a recovery group, a Bible study small group, and other groups. You were created to have a personal relationship with God, but not a private relationship with God. You need others, and others need you.

In addition to connecting with a group, you need a mentor—someone with more sobriety than you have. Scripture is full of such examples. David/Jonathan and Paul/Timothy come to mind immediately.

So here's your task for this week. Get with someone you know, who has more sobriety than you. You can visit with them over lunch or over the phone. Maybe you can schedule time before or after a recovery meeting. It's best to meet in person, if possible.

Ask them two questions: how they got sober and how they stay sober. Then journal below, reflecting on what you learn.

Person you will meet with: _____

When you will meet: _____

How they got sober: _____
_____
_____
_____
_____
_____
_____
_____
_____
_____

How they stay sober: _____
_____
_____
_____
_____
_____
_____
_____

WEEK 26
INVENTORY

"There is nothing noble in being superior to your fellow men.
True nobility lies in being superior to your former self."
—Ernest Hemingway

Empty Boxes

When I was about ten, my dad gave my brother and me a summer job. For a few hours a week, we went to his office to count inventory. Dad owned his own company, where he worked as a sales rep. He sold electronics components from major factories to companies all over the country. He also stocked some parts at his office, to fill smaller orders.

These capacitors and reed relays were stored in small boxes. And they had to be counted from time to time. That's where Jim and I came in.

Dad paid us $1 for every box that we counted. But I made the most money. While Jim would count the boxes with dozens of tangled small parts, I'd open the boxes, and if there were a lot of parts inside, I'd close them back up. I only counted the boxes that had one or two parts.

That's how most of us do our personal inventory. We count empty boxes. When we look inside and find the complexity of tangled parts, we quickly shut the box and move on.

Paul said, "Examine yourselves" (2 Corinthians 13:5).

We all need to take an honest inventory of ourselves from time to time. Patrick Henry said it brilliantly: "Whatever anguish of spirit it may cost, I am willing to know the whole truth, to know the worst and to provide for it."

It is when you open the box and begin to untangle the worst parts that you find truth, freedom, and lasting recovery.

It's time to open the box and untangle the mixed-up parts.

THIS WEEK'S EXERCISE
Peel an Orange

This week's exercise will be the tastiest one you will do all year. You need to buy, steal, or borrow an orange. Once you have your orange, you can proceed with this exercise.

Okay, have your orange? Follow these directions very carefully . . .

1. Peel your orange.
2. Eat your orange.

Hopefully, you were able to keep up. Now for the hard part. Your orange represents your life and personal recovery. Let me offer several points to this analogy.

First, what others see on the outside rarely matches what is on the inside. Think about it. If you had never seen the inside of an orange, would you have really known what it would look like once you peeled away the rind? Similarly, when others look at you, they are seeing the outside, not the inner struggles, pain, and addictions.

Second, you can't get to the good part until you peel away the cover. No one eats the rind. We peel it away and quickly discard it. It is what we find beyond the rind that matters. Likewise, no matter how damaged or bruised we may be on the inside, it is that inside—not our outer appearance—that matters most.

Third, getting to the heart of the orange is messy. Our hands get wet and sticky. But it's worth it, because the juicy orange segments beyond the rind bring satisfaction and pleasure. Now, let's apply the orange to your life.

1. How frustrated did you get trying to get to the "good part" of the orange? _____

   _____

2. What are the layers of your life that still need to be peeled back? _____

   _____

3. Are you willing to go through the messy process of peeling back your cover in order to find lasting recovery? What might that look like? _____

   _____

WEEK 27
SCRIPTURE

"That Book, sir, is the Rock on which
our Republic rests."
—Andrew Jackson

Ferrari vs. Pinto

A leading voice on the porn effects on millennials is Alex Lerza, founder and CEO of The Recovery Tribe. Lerza summarizes the struggle of teens and young adults with the illustration of a car. He says of the emerging generation, "When it comes to sex and porn, they have a Ferrari engine, a Pinto set of brakes, and no owner's guide."

King David prayed, "Do not remember the sins of my youth and my rebellious ways" (Psalm 25:7).

As a young man, David struggled with the same temptations of today's generation. (And it's not just *young* men.) So what do we tell this new generation of young people—with a Ferrari engine, Pinto brakes, and no owner's guide? I suggest two things.

First, we tell them sex is not bad. Too often, in our effort to keep our kids on the "straight and narrow," we rely on shame. "All sex before marriage is sin," we tell them. Since they have not yet been married, what they hear us saying is, "All sex is sin." We tie sex to shame. That's bad.

Second, we give them the owner's guide. The good news is that we have an excellent owner's guide. We teach them biblical principles. We tell them that sex is beautiful, that they are beautiful, and that the God of sex created it for them—in the right time.

Cut out the secrets and lift the veil. The way to guide your kids down the right path is not to remove their engine or add anti-lock brakes, but to introduce them to the owner's guide.

THIS WEEK'S EXERCISE
Try the SOAP Method

Scripture reading and memorization must become a vital part of your recovery. I suggest you purchase a Life Recovery Bible. Our ministry actually gives these away for free. But regardless of which Bible you use, you need to be in the Word. That's why I send my Recovery Minute devotion to men and women from 15 countries around the world. And that's why my second recovery book was a one-year devotional book for sex addicts.

One of the great recovery stories in the Bible is the story of the paralytic, who suffered for 38 years. His account is recorded in John 5:1-15. For this week's exercise, read that passage, then take notes, based on the SOAP method.

S = Scripture
O = Observations
A = Application
P = Prayer

Here's how it works. Write down the **Scripture** verse that speaks to you most loudly, from this passage. Then jot down a few pertinent **Observations** from this passage. Third, write a few points of **Application** from the passage. Finally, write out a **Prayer**, based on this study.

Scripture: _____

Observations: _____
_____
_____
_____
_____
_____
_____
_____

Application: _____
_____
_____
_____
_____
_____
_____
_____

Prayer: _____
_____
_____
_____
_____
_____
_____
_____

WEEK 28
DITCHES

Detours

Those who live in the north know just two seasons—winter and road repair. The harsh winter conditions bring ice and snow, which often buckle roads and create potholes. The result is that drivers in March and April are often faced with detours from their normal routes.

Some detours are the fault of the driver. A missed turn, lack of concentration, or refusal to ask for directions. They all mean rerouting our course. We take detours.

Barbara Bush said, "When you come to a roadblock, take a detour."

Zig Ziglar added, "Failure is a detour, not a dead-end street."

For many of us, our detour led us into a life of addiction. When we should have turned right, we went left. When we should have been in the Word, we were in the world.

But it's never too late to come back onto the main road. If you have driven off the intended path, there is an entrance ramp back to the thoroughfare of recovery. It's called "Jesus."

Jesus said, "I am the way" (John 14:6). Your habit has taken you off course. But it doesn't have to be a dead end. Follow Jesus back onto the road of sobriety and real recovery.

If you have drifted off course, it's not too late to get back on the main road. Follow Jesus. He is the only one who can take you where you want to be.

THIS WEEK'S EXERCISE
Define Your Ditch

In recovery, no matter how far you go down the road toward your goals, the ditch is still just as close on either side of the road. I have seen it happen far too often—a man with five, 10, or 15 years of sobriety falls to the temptations of illicit sexual activity.

It can happen so fast. An image, intrusive thought, memory, or some other trigger hits us in a weak moment, and we can fall. Let me be clear. *Any of us can fall—including you*! There are many ways to be ready and to stay sober. One important step is to recognize your weak spots. It is crucial to see the ditch on both sides of the road.

So here's the question of the day. If you fall, how will it happen? What are the two ditches that are the closest to your road today? And how do you plan to stay out of these two ditches?

Ditch #1: _____

How I plan to stay out of this ditch: _____

_____

_____

_____

_____

_____

Ditch #2: _____

How I plan to stay out of this ditch: _____

_____

_____

_____

_____

WEEK 29
CHOICES

"Life is a matter of choices, and every choice you make makes you."
—John Maxwell

Banquet of Consequences

We hear it all the time. "Life isn't fair." But is that really true?

It's not fair that you were emotionally abandoned by your parents. Abuse isn't fair. Neglect, family history, maltreatment—none of them are fair.

The American Psychiatric Association states that three million children experience abuse in America each year. The World Health Organization says this abuse comes in four forms: physical, sexual, emotional, and psychological. It's all abuse, and none of it is fair.

But at some point, we are responsible for our own decisions. What happens to us is not our fault. But our destructive responses are.

The prophet said, "The day of the Lord is near for all nations. As you have done, it will be done to you; your deeds will return upon your own head" (Obadiah 15).

Robert Louis Stevenson said, "Sooner or later, everyone sits down to a banquet of consequences."

Your choices bring a banquet of consequences. You can blame your past or you can change your future. Those are your two options.

THIS WEEK'S EXERCISE
Eat Some Starburst

You make your choices, then your choices make you. Decisions of your past—both good and bad—have become a part of your DNA. You can't go back. While you do get to write a whole new ending to your life, you cannot write a new beginning. One of the things we must learn in order to go forward is to quit trying to have a better past.

In recovery, we acknowledge our past and try to move on. But the abuse still happened. The trauma left enduring scars. The isolation shaped who we became. And then we, as addicts, fell into patterns that damaged us and those closest to us. But in recovery, we realize that God can use us this way, in ways he could not have used us otherwise.

This will be the tastiest exercise of the year. Buy a pack of Starburst candy. Then remove two of the individually wrapped candies. They must be of different flavors. Now, put these two together, and begin mashing them and twisting them until they become one. Keep working with the new product until the two colors are intertwined as one. This will take several minutes.

Once the two have become one, eat the new Starburst that is in your hand. Now, answer the following questions.

1. Which two flavors did you start out with?
_____ and _____

2. Once you meshed them into one, could you have separated them back into the two individual pieces that you started with? Why or why not? _____

_____

_____

3. Did the new product taste like either of the first two? __

_____

4. One candy represents you as a person. The other represents a choice you have made to act out in the past. In what ways did this choice change you permanently? _____

_____

5. Do you think good choices change who you become, as well? _____

WEEK 30
ACCOUNTABILITY

"People do what you inspect, not what you expect."
—Louis V. Gerstner, Jr.

Safety Net

Andy Stanley says the greatest question ever is: *What is the wise thing to do?* But the answer is not always clear. This leads to what Andy calls the second greatest question ever: *What do you think is the wise thing to do?*

Solomon said it like this: "Plans go wrong for lack of advice; many advisers bring success" (Proverbs 15:22). He also wrote, "There is safety in having many advisers" (Proverbs 11:14).

It's what I call the safety net. In recovery, none of us is as strong as all of us. Michael Leahy, founder of Bravehearts, says that only one man in 10,000 gets well on his own. We need each other.

To find successful recovery, you will need several people in your corner: a therapist, a pastor or priest, a sponsor, sponsees, 12-Step friends, and more.

When I am struggling, I call my pastor. Sometimes I call a mentor in the field of sex addiction. Other times, I call my sponsor.

The important thing is not who you call, but that you call. Can you surround yourself with helpful advisers and still slip or relapse? Absolutely! But if you go it alone, I can almost guarantee you will have a relapse. You need many advisers. That is about the best safety net you will ever find.

THIS WEEK'S EXERCISE
Get an Accountability Partner

I like to say it a lot—God will only heal what we reveal. There are two extremes to which I see recovering addicts run. They either (a) tell too many people their story, or they (b) tell their story to no one. Let's focus on that second extreme.

Many of us have cried out, "All I need is God!" And that sounds really good. The problem is that the God we need wired us for fellowship. More than that, we are wired for accountability. That's why the Bible promises healing when we confess our struggles to another human being.

There is usually that "one" magazine, website, computer file, TV show, or person. Because you tried to find victory on your own—and failed—you must now become accountable to one other human being.

You need an accountability partner. This is a person with whom you will meet regularly (weekly, if possible). You will tell him or her your struggles, slips, and temptations. You will give him or her permission to ask the tough questions about your daily sobriety. It will be best if this person meets the following criteria:

- He or she is the same sex as you.
- He or she is in recovery themselves.

- He or she can be trusted.
- He or she will pray for you.
- He or she offers godly wisdom.
- He or she is a committed Christ-follower.
- He or she will ask you the hard questions.

For this exercise, you need to do three things: (a) decide whom you will ask to be your accountability partner, (b) decide when you will ask him or her, and (c) actually ask him or her. Let's start with the first two parts of this assignment.

Who you will ask: _____

_____

When you will ask him or her: _____

_____

WEEK 31
DESPERATION

Lazarus

Hippocrates said, "Desperate times call for desperate measures." The man seemed to understand addiction. Desperation is the birthplace of recovery. You will never find lasting, sustainable recovery without it. You have to want recovery more than anything else.

I can't think of a more desperate situation in the Bible than that of Lazarus. The man was dying, so his sisters came to Jesus and pled for him to heal their brother. Jesus responded, "This sickness will not end in death" (John 11:4). And then, two days later, Lazarus died.

So what gives?

Notice what Jesus *did not say*. He didn't say Lazarus wouldn't die. He said the sickness would not *end in death*.

Think about it. If Jesus had healed Lazarus before he died, he would have just been another nameless guy in the Bible. What made Lazarus famous was not his healing, but his resurrection.

God is the master of the resurrection. Think about your own recovery. Your addiction may have killed your marriage, your job, your finances, and your self-esteem. But God's promise is that it won't end there. God always gets the final word.

Addiction brings death. But in death we find resurrection and recovery. When we rely fully on him, we discover that, as with Lazarus, "this sickness will not end in death."

THIS WEEK'S EXERCISE
What Are You Willing to Do?

Until you get desperate, you won't get well. I have yet to meet the person who achieved lasting sobriety casually. You can't sprinkle a little recovery work into your normal lifestyle and expect to get well. When I assess a new client, I can usually tell within a few minutes whether he will find success or not. It's all a matter of desperation. I see various levels on the desperation scale:

- "I may have a problem."
- "I have a problem."
- "This is an addiction."
- "I would like to get well."
- "I need help to get well."
- "I will work to get well."
- "I will be sick if I don't get well."
- "I'll die if I don't get well."

It is when we "hit bottom" that we get well. Why is this? Because we have to become desperate. Finding sexual sobriety is the hardest thing most of us will ever do.

For some, it requires attending 90 recovery meetings in 90 days. For most, it requires therapy. For all, it requires honesty and hard work.

If you are 90% in, you are 100% out!

What you do to find recovery is critical. But what matters even more is that which you are *willing to do*.

Here's a list. Check the things you are willing to do to get well, if they prove to be key components to your recovery plan.

_____ Do therapy

_____ Join a 12-Step group

_____ Complete this workbook

_____ See a C.S.A.T.

_____ Sell something to pay for therapy

_____ Work the 12 Steps

_____ Do a full clinical disclosure

_____ Take a polygraph

_____ Work with a sponsor

_____ Become a sponsor

_____ Get on Covenant Eyes

_____ Go to an inhouse treatment center

_____ Attend 90 meetings in 90 days

_____ Do nightly check-ins with your spouse

WEEK 32
GIVING BACK

"My own experience about all the blessings I've had in my life is that the more I give away, the more that comes back."
—Ken Blanchard

Father Damien

Tourists visit the Hawaiian Island of Molokai to enjoy the beaches and charm. But Father Damien came for a different reason. He came to help people die. You see, lepers came here first, starting in about 1840. They lived in isolation, on a tract of land set aside just for them.

When Father Damien heard of their plight, he begged with his supervisors to let him move to Molokai, to live with the lepers. The year was 1873. Damien said, "I want to sacrifice myself for the lepers."

Damien entered the world of the lepers. He dressed their sores, hugged their children, and buried their dead. Eventually, he would contract their disease. On April 15, 1889, Father Damien died of leprosy.

Father Damien did for the Molokai lepers what Jesus did for each of us. Not content to simply "treat" man, Jesus became a man. He joined the human race. The Bible says, "It was necessary for him to be made in every respect like us so that he could be our merciful and faithful High Priest before God" (Hebrews 2:17).

You can overcome every temptation because of what Jesus has done. Not content to look down on us from above, God has joined us. You are not alone. Because he became man, Christ knows exactly what you are going through, and he will walk with you every step of the way.

Recognize that you are not alone. Embrace the One who understands every temptation you will ever face—because he's been there. In fact, he still is.

THIS WEEK'S EXERCISE
Become a Sponsor

Helping others can be a vital part of your personal recovery from sexual addiction. This is what Step 12 is all about. As of this writing, I am sponsoring men (apart from this ministry) in five states. I always tell them, "I'm doing this for me." The fact is, when we help others, we help ourselves.

I hear something important in every 12-Step meeting. I pray the same will be true with the groups our ministry leads. But I also learn and grow by sponsoring other men. Dr. Doug Weiss writes, "Helping another struggling sex addict will strengthen your faith and remind you of the precious gift you have been given in your recovery."

The more you help others, the more you will be helped. You need to find ways to give back, to help others in their recovery. You can start by sponsoring someone else in their recovery work.

Pray and ask God to lay someone on your heart who needs your help. Then set a time to visit with them and make yourself available to lead them through their recovery process.

Date I prayed for God to lead me to someone in need: ____

_____

Names of three men I might help or sponsor:

1. _____

2. _____

3. _____

Date I will talk to one of these men: _____

WEEK 33
PRAYER

*"Prayer does not change God, but it
does change the person who prays."*
—Soren Kierkegaard

Driving Out Your Demons

The second Gospel tells the story of a boy possessed by demons. His father brought him to Jesus' disciples in hope that they would cast out the demons. But they failed to do so. So the man brought his son to Jesus, who cast out the demons. The disciples asked Jesus why they had failed in their efforts. Jesus offered a simple answer. "This kind can come out only by prayer" (Mark 9:29).

"Only by prayer," Jesus said.

Perhaps you can identify with the boy in this story. You feel like there is something inside of you that has a craving for which there is no answer. You have tried to overcome your addiction in many ways. At first, you ignored it. Then you downplayed it. Eventually, you came to recognize it as the adversary that it is. But you still didn't understand that this is a spiritual battle.

It's time to do what the disciples did. It's time to call in reinforcements, because "this kind can come out only by prayer." But the power isn't actually in the prayer; it's in the One to whom you pray.

Charles Spurgeon defined prayer like this: "True prayer is neither a mere mental exercise nor a vocal performance. It is far deeper than that—it is a spiritual transaction with the creator of heaven and earth."

If you recognize the nature of the opposition, you are ready to get well. It's time to pray.

You have worked as though it all depended upon you. Now pray as though it all depends upon God. Because it does.

THIS WEEK'S EXERCISE
Pray According to A.C.T.S.

The disciples of Jesus did not ask him how to pray. They pled, "Teach us to pray" (Luke 11:1). And then Jesus gave them what has become known as The Lord's Prayer. The point is not so much *how* we pray, but *that* we pray. Still, I hear it a lot. "I don't know where to start. I don't know how to pray."

So let me offer you an old, but powerful tool for your prayer life. This formula will help to keep your prayers balanced and on point. Try it now, and record your thoughts below.

It's called ACTS (as in the Book of Acts in the Bible). There are four parts to this prayer.

Adoration—Begin your prayer by expressing adoration to God for who he is. Focus on his character and attributes. Praise him for who he is.

Confession—Confess your sin to God, but more importantly, express your sins. Be specific. List your sins before the Lord, and ask him to forgive each one.

Thanksgiving—This is different from adoration. Rather than praising God for who he is (adoration), here you will thank God for what he's done. Be specific. Write out the things you are thankful for today.

Supplication—Now do what you already do when you pray, most times. Ask God for something. Ask for his blessings, wisdom, and healing. Pray for his intervention in your life, and pray for others.

It's time to pray! Write down the specifics of this prayer.

Adoration: _____
_____

Confession: _____
_____

Thanksgiving: _____
_____

Supplication: _____
_____

WEEK 34
ROUTINE

"I try to just focus on being in the same routine every single day."
—Patrick Mahomes

Holy Habits

Baseball Hall-of-Famer Al Kaline said, "You've got to develop good habits before the season begins. That way when the big play comes—and you never know when that will be—you will be ready."

Your sobriety tomorrow will be determined by what you do today. It's all about developing the right habits.

Camel Cigarettes knew this 50 years ago. They came out with an ad, in which they invited people to take the "30-day test." They asked people to try Camel for 30 days, knowing that by that time, they would be both loyal and addicted.

There was a man in the Bible who was the master of holy habits. His name was Daniel. When he was thrown to the lion's den, the king said, "May your God, whom you serve continually, rescue you!" (Daniel 6:16). King Darius had observed Daniel "distinguish himself by his exceptional qualities" (6:3) for 30 days—and longer. And it was the character developed by those habits—such as praying three times a day at the same place and time—that saw Daniel through.

Gandhi said, "Your actions become your habits, your habits become your values, and your values become your destiny."

Do you want sobriety tomorrow? Then develop holy habits today—prayer, Scripture reading, worship, meetings, recovery work. The more you do the right thing today, the harder it will be to do the wrong thing tomorrow.

Start developing one holy habit today in order to find real recovery tomorrow.

THIS WEEK'S EXERCISE
Plan a Routine

Practice makes perfect.

When I was 15, my Dad took me to the local miniature golf course every day on his way to work. I spent all of my allowance playing miniature golf that summer. By August, I got really good. I set the course record with a 27 (par 36), and won enough tournaments that I no longer had to pay to play. (With each tournament win came several free passes.) By the end of the summer, I had worked my way up the ranks into the adult division, and qualified for the state tournament. I finished in 4th place in the Texas State Putt-Putt Championship, sponsored by Coca Cola. I only missed 1st place by three strokes.

Practice makes perfect.

Yes, the Putt-Putt story is real. I still have a 3-inch trophy somewhere as proof. But aside from bragging on the greatest athletic achievement of my life, let me repeat the bigger point.

Practice makes perfect.

That is true when mastering a musical instrument, excelling academically, or reaching one's full potential in sports that are every bit as demanding as miniature golf.

And in recovery—practice makes perfect.

This week, focus on one recovery activity. Do it over and over. Make it a daily priority. Set a time and place to focus on this recovery activity. Some examples you might choose from are listed here:

- Read recovery material (this book will do)
- Pray
- Make a call
- Meditate
- Memorize the 3rd Step Prayer
- Journal

Set a time and place each day so you can be consistent. Commit to this daily activity. Make it a daily routine. Write your routine below, then stick to it every day this week.

My daily activity: _____

Day I will begin: _____

Place I will do this activity: _____

Time for this daily activity: _____

Check each day you follow this routine:

- Day 1 _____
- Day 2 _____

- Day 3 _____
- Day 4 _____
- Day 5 _____
- Day 6 _____
- Day 7 _____

WEEK 35
WORSHIP

The Saw

A man had a firewood factory that employed hundreds of men. He paid them well and gave them specific directions on what to do. But their work was slow and unproductive. Eventually, he had no choice. He fired the men and purchased a circular saw powered by a gas engine. In one hour, the new saw accomplished more than all the other men had done in a week.

The man asked his new saw. "How can you turn out so much work? Are you sharper than the saws my men were using before?"

The saw responded, "No, I am not sharper than the other saws. The difference is the gas engine. I have a stronger power behind me. I am productive because of the power that is working through me, not because my blade is stronger."

The man or woman who finds successful recovery doesn't do so because he or she has a sharper blade. It's all about the power within. The Bible calls that power the Holy Spirit.

Jesus promised his earliest followers, "You will receive power when the Holy Spirit comes on you" (Acts 1:8).

That's the secret. It's not the sharpness of the saw, but the presence of the Spirit. Ask God to empower your saw through the filling and power of the Holy Spirit.

THIS WEEK'S EXERCISE
Listen to 'Flawless'

In 2014, MercyMe came out with what has become my favorite song of this millennium. It's called *Flawless*. The song won the GMA Dove Award for Song of the Year and sat atop the charts for several weeks.

I love this line from the song:

"No matter the bumps, no matter the bruises, no matter the scars, still the truth is, The cross has made, the cross has made you flawless."

Bart Millard, lead singer, gives us the story behind the song. "Christ looks at you and says, 'You are the most amazing thing I've ever seen. In that sense, you are flawless.'"

Worship should be a frequent component of your recovery plan. Here's a great way to enter into worship this week. Listen to the song *Flawless*, then journal on how this song impacted you and spoke to your recovery.

You can easily find the song on YouTube. If you don't know how to do that, find anyone under 35, and they can help you! Listen to the song three times before you journal.

Date I listened to the song: _____

What this song says about God's grace: _____

_____

_____

_____

_____

_____

What this song says about my recovery: _____

_____

_____

_____

_____

_____

WEEK 36
LUST

Never Satisfied

Lust is progressive. It never satisfies. There's an old story about God's people returning from exile to Jerusalem. They started to rebuild the Temple, but when they faced opposition, they quit. In frustration, they turned inward, building lavish homes for themselves instead of furnishing God's House. For them, life was about taking the easy path and indulging in the pleasure of the moment.

In stepped a prophet named Haggai. He wrote, "Look what's happening to you! You have planted much but harvested little. You eat but are not satisfied. You drink but are still thirsty" (Haggai 1:5-6).

That is the picture of every addict. We eat, but are still hungry. We drink, but are still thirsty. There's a reason for this.

We are chasing temporary solutions to permanent problems.

I have acid reflux. It causes a burning in my esophagus. Sometimes, I do the right thing and drink a disgusting tasting liquid before bed. And I sleep all night. But other times, I eat a bowl of ice cream. Why? Because it tastes better in the moment. And it actually coats my throat, so it feels better for a few minutes. The problem is that in four or five hours, the pain returns and I end up having to drink the medicine anyway.

Every day, we are tempted to drink in the lust. And it feels good in the moment. But it only masks the real pain. What's the solution? Drink of the Living Water that never runs dry.

THIS WEEK'S EXERCISE
List Your Lust

Financial freedom experts like Dave Ramsey all suggest that before a person can get out of debt, he needs to know where he is spending his money. Clients are encouraged to journal for 30 days, to record all of their expenses. With that information, they can begin to put together a realistic budget.

The same idea applies to recovery. Whether you are trying to recover from a load of debt or a load of improper sexual activity, you need to know how bad the problem really is.

I love the SA definition of sobriety—achieving progressive victory over lust. If we only deal with our behaviors, we will never get well. The cycle of addiction tells us that we only do what we think. The genesis of acting out is lust. We must deal with our lust problem. But first, we have to measure the size and scope of that problem.

Max Dupree says the first job of every leader is to define reality as it really is. Likewise, the first task of the sex addict is to identify his struggle with lust as specifically as possible.

Ready for a painful and eye-opening exercise? List each occurrence of lust for the next seven days. You don't need to go into detail; just jot down a few words to identify the nature of each instance. Examples might be: "saw woman at the mall," "thought of a past partner," "lusted after woman on TV show," "objectified my wife."

Day 1
    a. _____
    b. _____
    c. _____

Day 2
    a. _____
    b. _____
    c. _____

Day 3
    a. _____
    b. _____
    c. _____

Day 4
    a. _____
    b. _____
    c. _____

Day 5
    a. _____
    b. _____
    c. _____

Day 6
    a. _____

    b. _____

    c. _____

Day 7
    a. _____

    b. _____

    c. _____

WEEK 37
SOWING

"Even after a bad harvest there must be sowing."
—Seneca

A Little Seed

"Will I ever get it?" "Will recovery ever stick?" "When the temptation hits, how will I know if I have what it takes to stay strong?"

I hear these questions all the time. Fortunately, we have an answer—from the lips of Jesus.

"Jesus said, 'The Kingdom of God is like a farmer who scatters seed on the ground. Night and day, while he's asleep or awake, the seed sprouts and grows, but he does not understand how it happens'" (Mark 4:26-27).

The farmer spreads his seed, then God takes over. The same principle works in recovery. If you take the actions of recovery, God will do a work that you cannot see. But when the battle hits, you will find that you have what it takes to win.

I do five miles a day on the treadmill. When I'm done, I get off right where I started. I haven't really gone anywhere. But the benefits are still there—better conditioning, more energy, and sore feet! Exercise today brings benefits tomorrow.

God took an orphan named Esther and put her in the right position to save his people. She didn't realize it at the time, but God was at work in her, to perform a higher purpose.

Joel Osteen says, "At this very moment, God is working behind the scenes in your life, arranging things in your favor."

Plant the seeds of recovery today, and you will be amazed at what God will do in your life—even when you don't see it.

THIS WEEK'S EXERCISE
Do a Random Act

The ultimate example of biblical giving is doing something for someone who cannot repay you, and while receiving no credit for your actions.

This week's focus will be sowing good seeds of recovery. You must invest your time and attention today in what you want to become tomorrow. This principle applies to all facets of the Christian life.

This week's exercise will call on you to sow a seed into the life of another person who cannot repay you. It's called a random act of kindness. There are many ways you can do this. Consider a few examples.

- Buy a recovery book for someone in your 12-Step group.
- Make a call to a friend who is new to recovery.
- Buy an inexpensive gift card for your sponsor.
- Do something kind for someone whom you have injured in the past.

- Send a small gift to a recovery ministry. (*There's Still Hope* accepts large gifts, as well!)
- Help set up for a meeting at your church this week.
- Bake cookies for a neighbor.
- Visit someone in a nursing home.

There is no limit to the things you can do to sow seeds of recovery. The amazing thing about recovery is that the more you give, the more you get back. Seeds are small, but they can make a huge difference in the life of the recipient—and the giver.

What will you do this week to sow a seed of recovery? __
_____
_____
_____
_____

WEEK 38
TRIGGERS

*"I'm an actor who believes we all have triggers to
any stage of emotion. It's not always easy to
find, but it's still there."*
—Hugh Jackman

"Danger, Will Robinson"

It was one of the great television shows of the 1960s—
Lost in Space. Every Wednesday night from 1965 to 1968,
I tuned in. If I missed *Lost in Space*, I lost my mind. For
those of you younger than me (about 95% of the world),
here's the synopsis. The show followed the ventures of
the Robinsons, a pioneering family of space colonists who
struggled to stay alive. CBS caught every moment.

Will Robinson was a teenage boy whose curiosity nearly cost him his life—in virtually every one of the 83 epi-
sodes. That's where the family robot came in. With three
words, he steered Will from the clutches of death.

"Danger, Will Robinson."

We all need to hear that voice in our head—"Danger."
When we begin to browse porn sites—"Danger!" When
we go to certain dating sites—"Danger!" When we go to
lunch with an attractive coworker—"Danger!" When we
put ourselves in compromising situations—"Danger!"

We have this promise: "The Lord will guard your going out and your coming in" (Psalm 121:8). He often does this with a still, small voice.

Listen for that voice. Listen for his warning. Recognize his message.

"Danger!"

Are you putting yourself in a position of great temptation? Then heed the voice of God—"Danger, Will Robinson."

THIS WEEK'S EXERCISE
H.A.L.T.!

We all have triggers—people, places, or predicaments that put us at the brink of a relapse. But there are four specific triggers that AA has been talking about for years. This simple formula has found its way into recovery material of all kinds, and is often used by therapists.

We are most vulnerable when we are **hungry**, **angry**, **lonely**, or **tired**.

1. Hungry

This is obvious. When we go without food, we become agitated. Our chemistry is off, and we seek to self-medicate. We want quick gratification. And too often, we find that in sex, rather than food.

2. Angry

Anger is a huge component of addiction. When we are angry at someone, resentment builds up. Anger is destructive. When we are angry at someone—even if it seems justifiable at the time—it only hurts us. An angry person thinks he deserves pleasure to even the score. And too often, he finds this in sex.

3. Lonely

When we are lonely, we tend to isolate. That always spells trouble, because we only stay sober within community. Rarely does a person act out except when he is alone—and lonely.

4. Tired

When we are overworked and don't get enough rest, we let our defenses down. To maintain sobriety requires diligence. God has created us for rest. To not get enough rest is to break one of the commandments. And it puts our recovery at risk.

Pick an exercise.

Exercise #1—Rate your personal H.A.L.T.

Which of these are your biggest challenges: hungry, angry, lonely, tired? _____

How are you tempted to act out by this trigger? _____

_____

_____

_____

_____

Exercise #2—People, places, predicaments

Give one example for each of these triggers in your personal life:

- People: _____
- Place: _____
- Predicament: _____

WEEK 39
OUTER CIRCLE

"The closer we get to the outer circle, the more
ground we will have to stay balanced."
—Siamrehab.com

Stay Close

It had been a great day. They were eye witnesses to the feeding of the 5,000. Now the disciples of Christ were riding high and they'd never look back, right? Wrong. We read, "That evening Jesus' disciples went down to the shore to wait for Jesus. But as darkness fell and Jesus still hadn't come back, they got into the boat and headed across the lake toward Capernaum. Soon a gale swept down upon them, and the sea grew very rough" (John 6:16-18).

We learn two lessons here. First, yesterday's victory is no guarantee of tomorrow's success. The disciples had just witnessed an amazing miracle. Surely, they'd stay on track now. But their newfound faith stayed with them for about two hours.

Second, it is important to wait on God. At the first sign of darkness and pending storms, the disciples left Jesus and went out on their own. They were willing to walk with him as long as they could do it on their own terms.

As a consequence, the disciples would have never made it to the other side of the lake, had Jesus not saved them—again. Henry Ford was right when he said, "Those who walk with God always reach their destination."

In recovery, life will be like that of the disciples. In the same day, they witnessed a great miracle and then encountered a harrowing storm. The key to survival is to never walk away from Christ.

When times are good, walk with Jesus. When times are bad, walk with Jesus. At all times—walk with Jesus.

THIS WEEK'S EXERCISE
Attend a New Meeting

Your outer circle activities are the things you do that contribute to your sobriety. These are areas where you need to strive for consistency, especially in the first year of your recovery. Here are some examples of typical outer circle activities:

- Prayer
- 12-Step work
- Family time
- Reading Scripture
- Meditation
- Recovery Day
- Church attendance
- Exercise
- Worship
- Therapy

Another outer circle activity is attending recovery meetings. It is possible to attend meetings and still not be sober. But it is nearly impossible to remain sober without attending meetings.

In Alcoholics Anonymous, there is an old expression that says, "There are three times when you should go to a meeting: when you don't feel like going, when you do feel like going, and at 8:00."

It is not a matter of how you feel. It is what you do that counts. Many, early in recovery, attend 90 meetings in 90 days. I found that to be very useful in my early recovery. These meetings provide insight, community, and encouragement. Your life may depend on attending meetings.

One of the things I have found most useful is to attend a new meeting every few weeks, either in my area or when I travel. This keeps my recovery from becoming stale and predictable.

Your first task is to find a "home meeting," one you are most committed to, if you have not done this already. You can find a local meeting easily. But for this week, your exercise is to attend a new meeting, or one you have not been to in at least three months. This can be a live meeting or a phone meeting. Here are a few websites that may help you find a meeting:

- Sexaholics Anonymous: sa.org
- Sex Addicts Anonymous: saa-recovery.org
- Celebrate Recovery: celebraterecovery.com
- Castimonia: castimonia.org
- 180 Recovery: 180recovery.com

Now, describe your feelings and experiences from this meeting, once you have attended, either in person or by phone. Try to identify at least one lesson you learned, which you can implement into your personal recovery plan.

The meeting I attended: _____

The date of the meeting: _____

One lesson or principle I learned at this meeting: _____
_____
_____
_____
_____

WEEK 40
20-MINUTE MIRACLE

"Count it all joy, my brothers,
when you meet trials of various kinds,
for you know that the testing of your faith produces steadfastness.
And let steadfastness have its full effect, that you may be
perfect and complete, lacking in nothing."
—James 1:2-4

The War Within

We often get this idea that the Apostle Paul had it all together, that he had risen above the common sins and temptations that derail the rest of us. Nothing could be further from the truth. Hear him in his own words:

"I know that good itself does not dwell in me, that is to say in my sinful nature. For I have the desire to do what is good, but I cannot carry it out" (Romans 7:18).

That is the war that rages within each of us. We want to do the right thing, but find ourselves coming up short. But I suggest that this struggle, of itself, is not a bad thing.

Frederick Douglass wrote, "Without a struggle there can be no progress."

So which side will win the battle? I suggest it is the side you feed the most. If you feed your addiction, expect a rough road ahead. But if you feed your recovery, expect success. And along the way, know that you will not likely win every battle.

Pope Paul VI said, "All life demands struggle."

Recovery may be the biggest struggle of all. But you only lose if you quit fighting. So stay in the fray, whether it feels like you are winning or not.

Engage the enemy today. Whatever the temptation, keep fighting. Feed your recovery with the things you know will work. Then keep at it. Eventually, freedom will be yours.

THIS WEEK'S EXERCISE
Practice the 20-Minute Miracle

One study estimated that the time span from when an addict feels a strong urge to act out and then actually does it is usually under ten minutes. We usually give in right away, or we stay strong. The exception is the man or woman whose primary acting out behavior involves paying for sex or meeting someone online. But even with them, the process begins quickly, as they go online or hop in their car to drive to a place where they should not go.

To those who feel like this urge is more than they can stand, I say three things.

1. What you feed, grows.

Sexual addiction is progressive. For example, if you masturbate today, you will likely be right back facing the same challenge tomorrow. And it only gets worse. There will be a time when what it took to satisfy your sexual appetite today is no longer enough.

2. Sex is not a need.

Someone once challenged me on this, insisting sex is a need. This was my response. I said, "I'm going to offer you four things. You can pick three of them for the next 30 days, but only three. You can have (a) food, (b) water, (c) oxygen, and/or (d) sex. Which one will you do without?" Here's the deal. You can't go 30 days without food, three days without water, or three minutes without oxygen. But you can go without sex. It is not a need.

3. If you can hold on for 20 minutes, you can hold on.

Within about 20 minutes after the dopamine rush, the urge will greatly diminish. You will no longer have the strong craving. If you can make it for 20 minutes, you can make it.

This 20-Minute Miracle has saved the sobriety of many of my clients. And it can be a huge tool in your toolbox, as well. But it is not enough to "white knuckle it" for 20 minutes. You need to distract your brain during this time. You need to refocus until the urge has diminished.

Below is a list of things you can do during these 20 minutes. Check the ones you will try. If, during this week, you find a need to practice this 20-Minute Principle, record your thoughts below.

20-Minute Checklist

_____ Pray
_____ Go for a walk
_____ Make a call
_____ Go for a drive
_____ Get with a nearby friend

_____ Read recovery material
_____ Cook a meal
_____ Read Scripture
_____ Engage in a hobby
_____ Go grocery shopping
_____ Quote Scripture
_____ Exercise

My reflections, having conducted this exercise: _____

_____

_____

_____

_____

_____

_____

_____

_____

_____

_____

_____

WEEK 41
SOLITUDE

*"Solitude is painful when one is young, but
delightful when one is more mature."*
—Albert Einstein

The Divorce of Marilyn Monroe

On January 21, 1962, Marilyn Monroe asked Judge Miguel Gomez for a plate of tacos and enchiladas. Then she filed for divorce from Arthur Miller, her third husband. One year later, she took her own life.

Born Norma Jean Mortenson, the "blonde bombshell" was a sex symbol, star of 24 movies, and had a wealth of $10 million at the time of her death at age 36. She had been married to Joe DiMaggio and had romantic ties to Marlon Brando and President John F. Kennedy. Monroe had fame and fortune. What she didn't have was peace.

At the height of her popularity, Monroe said, "I am trying to find myself. Sometimes, that's not easy." In another interview, the star admitted, "Dreaming about being an actress is more exciting than being one."

What do you dream about? If, like Marilyn Monroe, you are chasing pleasure, prepare to be disappointed. Solomon, talking to himself, concluded, "I said to myself, 'Come now, I will test you with pleasure to find out what is good.' But that also proved to be meaningless" (Ecclesiastes 2:1).

I asked a fellow sex addict, "Why do you act out?" He said, "That's simple. It brings me pleasure."

The problem is, pleasure only satisfies for the moment.

If, like Marilyn Monroe, you are trying to find yourself through pleasure, let me suggest this—find God first.

THIS WEEK'S EXERCISE
Sit on It!

The Bible never says, "Be loud and know that I am God." We all know we need to be still before God, but most of us stink at the follow-through. Ours is a world that puts a premium on activity. We work hard, play hard, and party hard. The last thing we make time for is solitude.

We know that Jesus went into the mountain, Paul went into the wilderness, and Moses went into the dessert. But we are more comfortable going into the office, the bar, or the gym. We like noise.

A friend sent me a comic strip recently. It told of a man whose wife convinced him to turn off the TV for one night. The man discovered—for the first time—that when turned off, the TV screen becomes black.

Don't worry. I'm not going to ask you to go to a monastery for a week. We'll start small. Give solitude a try for just 15 minutes.

Here's what you will do—*nothing*.

Am I going too fast for you? For 15 minutes, you will not watch anything, read anything, or say anything. You won't even pray, unless you consider silence a form of prayer. (It is.)

Plan a time and pick a place where you can sit and do nothing. It is important that this place be outside, where you can best experience the world as it was before God made big buildings and fast cars.

During these 15 minutes, simply enjoy the presence of God. Use all of the senses that he gave you. Afterward, jot down what you heard, saw, felt, smelled, and tasted of God and his presence.

Date of exercise: _____

Place of exercise: _____

How you experienced God and his presence:

- What you heard: _____
- What you saw: _____
- What you felt: _____
- What you smelled: _____
- What you tasted: _____

Summary: _____
_____
_____
_____

WEEK 42
HOUSECLEANING

*"I hate housework. You make the beds, you wash
the dishes, and six months later you have
to start all over again."*
—Joan Rivers

Taking Out the Garbage

John Piper tells the story about the time he had a fight
with his wife early in their marriage. He needed a break
from the argument, so he left the house to take the garbage
down the street to the pick-up spot. He says, "As I walked
down the driveway toward the street where we set the garbage, the sun broke through the morning clouds. To this
day, the profoundness of that moment grips me. Here I
was huffing and puffing with my hurt feelings and desires
for vindication, and God, who had every right to strike me
dead, opened the window of heaven and covered me with
pleasure. I recall stopping and letting it soak in. It felt like
paradise—garbage in hand."

The Bible says, "The heavens declare the glory of God;
the skies proclaim the work of his hands . . . In the heavens
God has pitched a tent for the sun" (Psalm 19:1, 4).

What was true for John Piper is also true for you and
me. We all have garbage we need to take out. We need to

take it to the cross, God's pick-up spot. That's where we lay our garbage down.

There is an interesting promise for those of us willing to release our garbage. We experience God's glory and his redeeming grace in the process. God does not wait until we are garbage-free to reveal his glory. He has "pitched a tent" of blessing for each of us who are in the process of taking out the garbage.

What garbage have you been hanging onto? It's time to let it go. Then prepare for the blessing in the journey, not just the destination.

We all have garbage to take out. Start bagging it up today, then take it to the cross. And prepare to meet God along the way.

THIS WEEK'S EXERCISE
Clean House

We have some dear friends who have a home in our city of Bradenton, Florida. But this is not their primary residence. When they are not here, we sometimes go by the house for them, to make sure everything is working. We check the lightbulbs, faucets, toilets, etc. And when someone has been staying at the house, we take out the trash.

In most neighborhoods, "regular" trash is picked up a couple of days a week. Recycled trash is picked up on another day. But in order for the trash guys to pick it up, we have to haul it to the curb. They won't walk through your front door and rummage through your house looking for your trash. That would be creepy.

You may want them to take your trash away, as far as the east is from the west—to never be seen again. But until you make the effort to haul it to the curb, your trash isn't going anywhere. And the longer you hang onto it, the more it will stink.

In recovery, you need to clean house from time to time. You need to take out your "trash." This trash comes in many forms:

- Old letters
- Old pictures
- Old devices
- Old magazines
- Old web links
- Hidden cash
- Hidden phone numbers
- Hidden email addresses

In a sense, you need to destroy your old trash. But what you really need to do—on a spiritual level—is to take your trash to the curb. Let God destroy it. Yes, you need to get rid of the materials you are holding onto. But you also need to confess your trash to God in prayer, with a repentant heart. Let's get started.

Getting rid of the physical evidence:

- _____
- _____
- _____
- _____
- _____

Confessing the hidden "trash" of your heart:

- _____
- _____
- _____
- _____
- _____

WEEK 43
CONFESSION

*"Sacrifice, discipline, and prayer are essential. We gain
strength through God's Word. And when we fumble
due to sin – and it's gonna happen – confession
puts us back on the field."*
—Lou Holtz

The Tell-Tale Heart

Edgar Allan Poe's short story, *The Tell-Tale Heart*, tells
the gruesome story of a murderer who hides his victim's
body under the floorboards of his house. He is so confident that he cannot be discovered that he invites police
investigators into his house, where he cheerfully answers
all of their questions, while standing just above the corpse.

Then the murderer hears the sound of a beating heart
from below his feet. He wonders why the police don't
seem to hear it, as the beating gets louder. Though the of-
ficers know nothing, the man finally loses it and confesses
his crime.

Geoffrey Chaucer said, "The guilty think all talk is of
themselves." In other words, the guilty become consumed
in the destitution of their souls.

The Bible says, "Whoever conceals his sins does not
prosper, but the one who confesses and renounces them
finds mercy" (Proverbs 28:13).

John Adams said, "Great is the guilt of an unnecessary war."

One of the most unnecessary wars is the one that rages in the heart of a man who has something to hide. A man is crippled by his guilt and buried by his secrets. The key to recovery is not living a sin-free life. It is outing our mistakes before they destroy us.

THIS WEEK'S EXERCISE
Write a Deathbed Confession

Are you ready for a morbid exercise? Well, we have one for you! First, the background.

Confession is good for the soul. King David said it like this: "I gave an account of my ways and you answered me" (Psalm 119:26). David knew what many of us have yet to understand—God can only heal what we reveal.

Is there anything you are still holding onto? Is there anything you have yet to get out, to confess to God and another human being? No one will see this exercise, unless you choose to share it with them. This is only meant to be between you and God.

If you were on your deathbed, I'm guessing you would want to make sure everything was right between you and God. You wouldn't want there to be any unconfessed sin. So this is your chance. Write a deathbed confession to God—telling him anything you have been holding onto.

My Deathbed Confession

Dear God, _____

_____

_____

_____

_____

_____

_____

_____

_____

_____

_____

_____

_____

_____

WEEK 44
MONEY

Money Trap

I learned something from my 30 years as a senior pastor. People act funny when you talk about money. But money matters—a lot. John Wesley said, "Make all you can, save all you can, and give all you can." Woody Allen mused, "Money is better than poverty, if only for financial reasons." And Jerry Seinfeld observed, "Dogs have no money. Isn't that amazing? They're broke their entire lives, but that never steals their joy."

Money—or lack thereof—steals a lot of joy.

What does this have to do with addiction? Dr. Elizabeth Hartley explains, "Financial problems are often a symptom of behavioral addictions."

I can relate to the man who lamented, "I'm so poor, there's a kid in India with my picture on his refrigerator."

But it's true. What you do with your money says a lot. That's why Paul warned, "Those who want to be rich fall into temptation, a trap, and many foolish and harmful desires, which plunge people into ruin and destruction. For the love of money is a root of all kinds of evil, and by craving it, some have wandered away from the faith and pierced themselves with many griefs" (1 Timothy 6:9-10).

Having money is not sinful. Many heroes of the Bible had money: Abraham, Jacob, Job, David, Solomon, Lydia, Joseph of Arimathea. And that's okay; the problem is when money has you. So learn to enjoy money—but don't crave it, for that is a sign of addiction.

THIS WEEK'S EXERCISE
Follow the Money

Being accountable for their finances has saved many sex addicts from acting out and losing their freedom and family. The following techniques can stop several forms of acting out instantly. For many, most acting out behaviors require money. Money is what makes the sick, illicit sexual world go around. Without money, even in the addict's lost desperate emotional state, he cannot purchase anything. Accountability and money can save your sobriety.

How this can be practiced is a very individual matter. Below, you will read some methods for financial accountability that you should find very helpful. These are practices you can start this week, and then carry forward. Typically, it takes six to twelve months to establish enough sobriety to begin to loosen some of these parameters.

Check the specific strategies you will engage, starting this week:

_____ Limit credit card use and show statements to your spouse.

_____ Use checks instead of credit cards and review your bank statement with your spouse.

_____ Eliminate any separate bank accounts.

_____ Carry a limited amount of cash, perhaps under $20.

_____ Do not hide any cash.

_____ Keep receipts for all expenditures.

_____ Review any spending with your spouse at the end of each day.

_____ Other: _____

_____ Other: _____

_____ Other: _____

WEEK 45
AMENDS

*"If actions were always judged by their consequence,
we'd spend half our lives making amends."*
—Luke Skywalker

Restitution

Restitution—it's something we don't talk about much, and we do it even less. But restitution is a key to recovery. Restitution is a biblical word for making amends. And the concept is rooted in the Law of Moses.

One of the earliest writings of the Law includes a passage on making restitution.

"They must confess the sin they have committed. They must make full restitution for the wrong they have done, add a fifth of the value to it and give it all to the person they have wronged" (Numbers 5:7).

God provided clear steps for those who have violated others. These steps include admitting the wrong things we have done and providing restitution wherever possible. If we follow these simple steps, we will make significant progress toward recovery.

There are three ways to make amends.

First, we can make direct amends—to the person we have offended, in an effort to make things right. Sometimes, it is not possible or wise to contact the offended party. In these cases, we can make indirect amends—doing things for someone else. Finally, we can make living amends—making a lifestyle change.

It's all about restitution. In recovery, we seek to make things right. In the process, God makes us right.

THIS WEEK'S EXERCISE
Make Amends

In 12-Step work, we don't make amends until the 9th Step. And that's a problem. It is not healthy—for us or the other person—to wait too long to make amends. And that was never the intent by the authors of the 12 Steps. They actually meant for the Steps to be completed in 30 days.

If you are in a healthy place, regardless of where you are in your Step work, now is a good time to make amends. Your spouse or child shouldn't have to wait several months to hear your remorse, apology, and intent to live a better life.

By the time you have come to this exercise, you have probably already been in recovery for a while. You may have completed my 90-Day Recovery Guide or some lesser plan (humor intended). So you have likely already made some amends.

We will not try to get into the details of making amends here. For that, I suggest reading my 90-Day Recovery Guide or other literature. For this week's purposes, let's not make this too difficult. Ask God to impress you with the name of one person to whom you can make amends, and then schedule a time to do this. Your amends should be in writing, and read to this person. Write a rough draft below.

Name of the person to whom I will make amends: _____
_____

My relationship with this person: _____

When I will attempt to make amends:: _____

I did it! These are my reflections on making amends with this person: _____
_____
_____
_____
_____
_____
_____

Rough Draft of My Amends

_____
_____
_____
_____
_____
_____
_____
_____
_____
_____
_____
_____
_____
_____
_____
_____
_____
_____

WEEK 46

PERSISTENCE

"Great works are performed not by strength, but by perseverance."
—Samuel Johnson

Stay at It

Charles Schultz debuted his first-ever Peanuts comic strip on October 2, 1950, in nine newspapers around America. Over the next six decades, Schultz produced 18,000 more comic strips. The wisdom of Charlie Brown, Lucy, Linus, and the whole gang has guided many of us through the challenges of life.

One of those challenges—especially for those of us in recovery—is to stay at the hard work necessary to find success. We give up too early.

Lucy has the answer. "If no one answers the phone, dial louder."

Paul said it like this. "To those who by persistence in doing good seek glory, honor and immortality, he will give eternal life" (Romans 2:7).

One day a young lady was driving with her dad in the passenger seat. They encountered a bad storm. She noticed that several cars had pulled over because of the severity of the storm. She asked, "Should I pull over?" Her dad said to keep driving. The storm got worse, and more cars pulled over. "Should I pull over now?" asked the young driver. "No, keep driving," said her dad. Eventually, they emerged from the storm. "Now pull over," said the father. "Why now?" asked his daughter. "So you can look back at all the people who gave up and are still in the storm."

The fact is, the road to recovery will encounter many storms. The answer is not to pull over, but to keep driving. It's about persistence. It's about determination.

THIS WEEK'S EXERCISE
Draw a Picture

You need to do two things to stay sober: (a) start recovery work, and (b) continue recovery work. I wish the need for recovery work just went away. I would love to tell you that this problem will go away. For a few, it actually does. But that is rare. For most of us, this principle rings true—what it took to get us healthy, it will take to *keep* us healthy.

The word for the week is this—persistence.

While it's true that you may be able to back off some (no need for 90 meetings in 90 days forever), it is better to do too much recovery work than not enough.

Bud Wilkinson, the old football coach at Oklahoma, once looked up at 90,000 fans who were yelling down to the field, and said, "We have thousands of fat people in the stands telling us how to do our jobs."

To stay sober, you have to stay on the field of play. You can't let up.

For this week, you can pick between two exercises. One requires drawing, but don't let that scare you. Your work will not be graded. The other exercise will be more comfortable for those who see life as a bunch of lists.

Exercise #1

Draw a picture of what life will look like in five years, if you remain consistent in your recovery work. Be as creative as you can. Do the drawing in the space below.

Exercise #2

Make a list of the things you will commit to doing consistently for the next five years.

_____

_____

_____

_____

_____

_____

WEEK 47
ANGER

All the Rage

Most addicts have anger issues. Some of us have a history of rage, so we try to stifle our feelings. Others stuff their feelings of anger, pretending they don't exist. Why? We were never allowed to express these feelings in the past. Evaluating our anger and how to deal with it appropriately is an important part of our recovery.

We are warned in Scripture to be "slow to anger" (James 1:19).

Why is this important in recovery? Because anger leads to bitterness, and bitterness leads to fall. Our anger hurts those around us, but it mostly hurts us.

Ralph Waldo Emerson wrote, "For every minute you remain angry, you give up sixty seconds of peace of mind."

That's sixty seconds you cannot afford to give up.

Early in my recovery, I was angry toward those who contributed to my childhood isolation. I was angry toward family, neighbors, friends—and God. Especially God. But through therapy and growth, I learned to deal with my anger. It's not that anger ever really goes away, but it can be managed. Let's rephrase that. *It must be managed.*

THIS WEEK'S EXERCISE
Rate Yourself

A friend who has been a counselor for 35 years told me that he believes that anger is at the root of all addiction. That made me mad! Now, I'm no psychologist, and I certainly don't have the training necessary to either support or refute my friend's analysis. But we all know that anger is a huge component of addiction. This anger may be directed at ourselves, someone else, or even God. And we all have it—on some level.

When I hear anger in an addict's voice, I know what is probably coming next. Relapse follows anger like wet follows rain. They are pretty hard to separate.

So let's dig a little deeper. Think about a recent bout with anger, then journal about how it affected your sobriety, below.

Date of your anger: _____

How much anger did you feel (scale of 1-10)? _____

What happened to make you angry? _____
_____
_____
_____
_____
_____
_____

_____

_____

_____

_____

Did you act out sexually as a result? _____

How did you feel after this bout with anger? _____

_____

_____

_____

_____

_____

_____

_____

What are you going to do differently the next time you feel
anger coming on? _____

_____

_____

_____

_____

_____

WEEK 48
REGRETS

Cat's in the Cradle

When the Bible speaks of a father's sin affecting the second and third generation, this was because in those days, three generations lived together. Our children become who we are, not who we want them to be.

In his iconic song, *Cat's in the Cradle*, Harry Chapin wrote this famous last stanza:

I've long since retired and my son's moved away.
I called him up just the other day.
I said, "I'd like to see you if you don't mind."
He said, "I'd love to, dad, if I could find the time.
You see, my new job's a hassle,
And the kids have the flu.
But it's sure nice talking to you, dad.
It's been sure nice talking to you."
And as I hung up the phone, it occurred to me,
He'd grown up just like me.
My boy was just like me.

Attend any 12-Step meeting, and you will hear something like this: "I discovered my dad's pornography when I was nine years old." The fact is, our kids are watching—and learning. Keep that in mind the next time you are tempted to act out.

Our children will tend to be like us, not like we want them to be. So take one step today to become the person you want them to be.

THIS WEEK'S EXERCISE
Face Your Regrets

Anyone who says they have no regrets hasn't lived very long. Or their memory is really bad. Or they have a heart of stone. We all have regrets. We have things we wish we could do over. I've never met a person who, if he could live his life over, wouldn't change a thing.

The problem with regrets isn't that we have them, but that we haven't learned from them. Our regrets can be really good teachers. The only way your past mistakes win is if you let them. Any experience we learn from can be turned into a positive. When Paul promised that "all things work together for good to those who love God" (Romans 8:28), he didn't limit these things to "good things." He said, "all things."

List three regrets of your past, and more importantly, what you can learn from them or how you can make them right.

Regret #1: _____

What I can learn from it or do to fix it: _____
_____

Regret #2: _____

What I can learn from it or do to fix it: _____
_____

Regret #3: _____

What I can learn from it or do to fix it: _____
_____

WEEK 49
REALIGNMENT

"To improve is to change; to be perfect is to change often."
—Winston Churchill

Charlie Brown

Charlie Brown commented on what it meant to have a good day. "I know it's going to be a good day when all the wheels on my shopping cart turn the same way."

If ever there was a time when our lives needed to be in alignment, it is in our personal recovery. That means having all our wheels headed in the same direction—therapy, meetings, prayer, working the Steps, calling our sponsor, surrender, honesty. If we try to maintain sobriety with even one of the wheels out of alignment, we will live a life of constant frustration.

The good news is the road to recovery is well-lit. "The Lord says, 'I will guide you along the best pathway for your life'" (Psalm 32:8). God is committed to your personal recovery.

Martin Luther King, Jr., said, "Faith is taking the first step, even when you don't see the whole staircase."

When I got into recovery, I didn't see the whole staircase. But I always saw the next step. And that is enough.

Be proactive. Do the things that keep your cart headed in the right direction. Follow God's plan for your life—one day at a time.

THIS WEEK'S EXERCISE
Listen to This

From time to time, it is wise to reevaluate our recovery. Are we on the right track? Have we fallen into a rut? Are we still growing in our spiritual walk? Are we still moving forward in our sobriety? Have we learned anything new that can help us maintain recovery for life?

It is good to listen to a new voice occasionally. One way to do that is by listening to a podcast on recovery. There are many options available. I will list a few ministries that provide excellent podcasts. Feel free to find your own podcast. After you listen to this podcast, write your reflections below. Look for one significant lesson or principle that applies to your own recovery.

Podcasts that will bless your recovery:

- Pure Sex Radio (2.bebroken.com)
- Castimonia (castimonia.org)
- Porn-Free Radio (recoveredman.com)
- Carol the Coach (sexhelpwithcarolthecoach.com)
- XXXChurch (xxxchurch.com)
- Bethesda Workshops (bethesdaworkshops.org)
- Prodigal's International (prodigalsinternational.org)

Date I listened to a podcast: _____

The podcast I listened to: _____

Lessons/principles I heard that will help my personal recovery:

_____
_____
_____

WEEK 50
PATIENCE

"He that can have patience can have what he will."
—Benjamin Franklin

Learn from the Snail

Nineteenth century preacher Charles Spurgeon taught what he called "the lesson of the snail." He said, "By perseverance the snail reached the ark."

Nothing will bring you victory over lust like perseverance. Never give up. Failure is the path of least persistence.

Consider the honey bee. To produce one pound of honey he must visit 56,000 clover heads. Since each head has 60 flower tubes, he must make 3.36 million visits to produce one pound of honey.

A Little League baseball team trailed by 21 runs entering the bottom of the first inning. Still, one of the players remained confident. "Why are you so optimistic?" a coach asked.

"It's simple," said the boy. "We haven't batted yet."

Lust. A second look. Fantasy. We all battle these temptations—and more. And none of us has been victorious every time. But that's okay. The key to victory is perseverance. Stay in the battle. Keep swinging.

Your job is simple. Do the next right thing. Then do that again tomorrow. Take small steps—one day at a time.

Paul said it like this: "Never tire from doing the right thing" (2 Thessalonians 3:13).

Think of yourself as the snail and the ark as recovery. You can get there. It won't be easy and it won't come fast. But it can happen—if you have perseverance.

THIS WEEK'S EXERCISE
Get Two Chairs

We often become impatient with our recovery. Everyone wants to be recovered, but no one wants to be *recovering*. With time, it gets easier. The euphoric recall, fantasies, and triggering thoughts slowly diminish. We develop new habits and become stronger. With each small step forward, we find ourselves progressively overcoming our worst demons.

Recovery cannot be rushed. It is a marathon, with a lot of hurdles along the way. But recovery will come if we stay at it.

You can be light years ahead of where you are now, in one year. But that will only happen if you make wise choices now. You can't just wake up one day and live in freedom any more than you can wake up one day—50 pounds overweight—and decide to run a marathon that afternoon.

To be well in one year, you must focus on the things you can do today. This exercise will require four things:

- Two chairs
- A quiet room
- This workbook
- A pen

Get that set up, and you can go to work.

Step 1—Sit in one of the chairs, facing the other chair, with this workbook in hand.

Step 2—Write down five things you will change in the coming year. These may include doing 12-Step work, joining a group, reading a book, getting on Covenant Eyes, getting a sponsor, seeing a therapist, or going through my 90-Day Recovery Plan. Get creative. Write this down below.

_____

_____

_____

_____

_____

_____

Step 3—Imagine your life in one year, if you complete all of these five tasks. Now go sit in the opposite chair—which represents your life in one year—and thank God in advance for what is to come.

WEEK 51
MEMORIES

"One of the keys to happiness is a bad memory."
—Rita Mae Brown

Short Memories

One of our biggest problems is that we have short memories. We are like the guy whose wife made him dinner every night for their entire 50 years of marriage. The next day, he asked her, "Who's cooking dinner tonight?"

God has been cooking your dinner for a long time. He has proven his faithfulness over and over. But too often, you have pulled a Rehoboam. The Bible says of the young king, "After Rehoboam's position as king was established and he had become strong, he and all Israel with him abandoned the law of the Lord" (2 Chronicles 12:1).

G.K. Chesterton recorded the following dialogue.

Father Brown: "There is one great spiritual disease."

Flambeau: "And what is the one great spiritual disease?"

Father Brown: "Thinking one is quite well."

I love the words of the old 18th century hymn, written by Isaac Watts. "When I survey the wondrous cross, on which the Prince of Glory died, my richest gain I count but loss, and pour contempt on all my pride."

One of the keys to lasting recovery is to take nothing for granted. Watch out for pride. Never forget the danger of thinking you are quite well.

THIS WEEK'S EXERCISE
Get a $10 Bill

Shame. It fills the heart of every addict. And until shame is eradicated, the addiction will generally persist, because shame says, "You are a bad person." The addict's natural response to shame is, "Well, if I'm who you say I am, I might as well continue in my destructive behaviors."

Shame is tied to memories of all the bad things we have done or thought. These memories will kill us if we let them. It is critical that we understand that no matter the damage we have done to ourselves and others, we are still the redeemable creation of God. While our past may limit many opportunities for future service to the kingdom, other options will begin to open up.

Here's the deal—there is nothing you have ever done that will make God love you less.

And there's more good news—you aren't big enough to thwart God's ability to use you. At no time does God say, "Bummer! Now my son has crossed that line, and I don't know how I can ever use him again."

Here's your exercise for this week. Get ahold of a $10 bill. Any bill will work, actually, but we'll go for a $10 bill because God says you're still a "10," no matter what you've done in your past.

There are two parts to this exercise.

First, take that bill and wad it up. Bend it, fold it, roll it. Create as many creases in that $10 bill as you can.

Second, unfold the bill. Straighten it out. Now, answer the following questions.

1. Is it possible to remove all the creases and make the $10 bill look brand new again? Why or why not?

_____

2. How much was the bill worth before you wadded it up?

_____

3. How much is it worth now?

_____

4. What is the lesson of the $10 bill? How does this apply to your life? _____

_____

_____

WEEK 52
DOMINOES

"The domino effect has the capacity to change the course of an entire world."
—J.D. Stroube

Fun in Kansas

When we visited my grandparents' home in Kansas when I was a child, we spent hours playing dominoes. But I quickly found a better use for these numbered rectangles. I would collect as many of them as possible, then set them up on a large table, so that when I knocked one over, the rest would eventually fall.

It was fun to tap the first domino over, then run to the other end of the line and wait for the last one to fall. For several seconds, the last domino stood firm. But I always knew what would ultimately happen. It was going down.

That's how addiction works. Many a man or woman has relapsed by paying a prostitute, viewing pornography, masturbating, or committing some other inappropriate sexual act. When that act is over, we can't believe what just happened, and we respond in shame.

But we miss the point. The act itself is simply the last domino to fall. It is the inevitable result of a process we put in place with the first domino—a quick fantasy, a moment of lust, a flirtatious gesture. If we are to avoid future relapses, we must learn to focus on the first domino more than the last.

When Eve was confronted by God over her first sin, she said, "The serpent deceived me, and I ate" (Genesis 3:13). Eve missed the point. She left out the first domino. She only ate the forbidden fruit because she chose to listen to the serpent in the first place. She could only be deceived because she chose to listen.

THIS WEEK'S EXERCISE
Let's Play Dominoes

I'm going to guess that you didn't wake up one day and decide to become a sex addict. For most of us, it took years to get as messed up as we became. Addiction is the predictable result of trauma, isolation, abuse, bad choices, psychological issues, and much more. None of us will ever really know all of the components that contributed to making us who and what we are.

But most of the ingredients to our addiction are pretty clear. And they didn't all happen at once. Addiction is the culmination of events and circumstances that have taken their toll over decades of our development.

Dominoes can be used to play a game that features numbers. Or they can be set up on a table in a way that allows all of them to fall—if just one of them falls.

To find lasting freedom, you need to deal with some of the individual dominoes that have fallen in your past. Identify them below.

Childhood dominoes:

- _____
- _____
- _____

Trauma dominoes:

- _____
- _____
- _____

Abuse dominoes:

- _____
- _____
- _____

Isolation dominoes:

- _____
- _____
- _____

Relational dominoes:

- _____
- _____
- _____

Other dominoes:

- _____
- _____
- _____

TEN RULES OF RECOVERY

Congratulations! You have just completed a rigorous period of recovery that will set you up for a lifetime of success. But remember, the work doesn't stop here. It's what you do next that will determine your future. You can walk in freedom from sexually compulsive activities for the rest of your life, one day at a time.

I encourage you to do two things, going forward. First, stay in a group. If you have been in one of my Freedom Groups, I hope you will keep coming back! If you are a part of some other group, keep going. You never graduate from recovery. In every meeting, you have something to learn. So stay in the fight. You are worth it!

Second, give back. If you'd like to lead others through my 90-Day Recovery Program, let me know. Perhaps God wants you to share your story, sponsor others, or write a book. One thing is for sure. What God allows, he redeems. Your story should not be kept silent. You can help others, and in the process, secure your own recovery.

One of the blessings of leading a ministry like ours is the training I have received and the hundreds of men and women we have met. I'm still learning – every day. But I want to leave you with a few things I've already learned. I call them my "Ten Rules for Recovery." I hope you'll take time to reflect on each one.

May God bless you as we continue this journey together . . .

Rule #1

God loves me more than he hates my mess.

Rule #2

No matter how far I go down the road of recovery, the ditch is still just as close.

Rule #3

The opposite of addiction is not sobriety, but community.

Rule #4

Yesterday's victory is no guarantee of tomorrow's success.

Rule #5

Recovery is about direction, not destination.

Rule #6

What I think today, I'll do tomorrow, and become the day after that.

Rule #7

Free cheese is always available in the mousetrap.

Rule #8

I am crippled by my addiction, but buried by my secrets.

Rule #9

I won't commit to a lifetime, just for a day.

Rule #10

God isn't going to use me despite my past, but because of it.

www.ingramcontent.com/pod-product-compliance
Lightning Source LLC
Chambersburg PA
CBHW060752050426
42449CB00008B/1370